# MY LIFE IN THE SHADOW WORLD:

## Reflections of a Television Showrunner

Todd Slavkin

ISBN: 9798620853915

# CONTENTS

# INTRODUCTION

As a child growing up in the suburbs of Los Angeles, I used to walk to the local library after school and head straight to the Young Adult section, where I plucked book after book from the shelf and read the afternoon away until my mom picked me up after she got off work. This one-story brick building was my cathedral, and the place where I began to gorge myself on character driven fiction, the more highly charged emotional storytelling the better. Judy Blume was my jam and I wasn't afraid to admit it. I also liked to write - short stories, little plays, a novella called "The End of Life" when I was 11 after my Grandmother died. But reading was and still is one of my favorite past-times.

Back then I wasn't into reading anything that remotely resembled nonfiction, except for one specific genre. The books that chronicled the making of movies or music. It began with my obsession over the movie JAWS. I was in fifth grade and the movie had taken over the cultural landscape. My parents thought I was too young to go see it, so to prove to themselves, and myself, that I was capable of handling the horror, I read the novel, which of course terrified me much to my delight. If that wasn't enough, I found a book in the library titled The Jaws Log, written by Carl Gottlieb (Dell, 1974), an expertly detailed behind the scenes account of the making of the movie written by the screenwriter. I ate up every single word. It was mesmerizing. It would end up having a huge impact on my life, and give my mom the knowledge that I now knew everything there was to know about Jaws and I couldn't possibly be traumatized by watching the movie. Weeks later I finally got to go to the theater to see Jaws, which was even better than I ever imagined, and I continued reading every "making of" book I could get my hands on.

In Ms. Kvitky's sixth grade science class at Palms Junior High, I met Darren Swimmer and instantly recognized a kindred soul. He too was a writer and voracious reader as well as a talented piano player. We became fast friends, and as I began to learn bass guitar (Paul McCartney was my inspiration) we started to write songs together for our new-wave band BLANK EXPRESSION, performing gigs throughout high school at The Troubadour and other clubs in Los Angeles. Darren was/is an incredible musician, a film music major during college who scored my short films when I was in film school. Our collaboration continued when we wrote a movie script together in my parent's study for two weeks straight, day and night, fueled by an endless amount of creative energy. We sold that script to David Geffen's film company in 1990 for enough money to quit our day jobs. Thirty years later, our friendship and career has endured enough drama for a lifetime of telenovelas, but we are still standing and get along fairly well.

Throughout my career in film and television, I always wondered if I would ever end up working on a project that would be worthy of a "making of" book. Sure my career has been jam packed with dramatic, strange, hilarious, exciting, depressing, beautiful and tragic moments that could fill endless amounts of pages. Right after graduating college I was lucky enough to sell my first screenplay, "Paging Mr. President" written with Eddie Tahaney, in 1987 to 20th Century Fox at the tender, naive age of 21, and stupid enough not save any of the money for taxes (thank you Aunt Vann for the loan to the IRS). After selling our first screenplay, Darren and I embarked on a twelve year screenwriting career selling movie scripts and pitches. Two of them were produced but neither made it into theaters (unless you count a test screening we had at an AMC theater that was a glorious once-in-a-lifetime experience).

Our entry into television writing was a sample episode for SIX FEET UNDER we wrote on spec to try and garner interest in us from the television industry. We were fortunate to get hired by Al Gough & Miles Millar on SMALLVILLE as executive story editors in season two. Seven seasons later we were promoted to showrunners with Kelly Souders & Brian Peterson, our brother and sister from another mother who started on the show the same time we did and remain close friends to this day. The reboot of MELROSE PLACE was the first pilot we wrote, and we have gone on to run many other shows we are incredibly proud of -- shows that were their own amazing adventure. But who would really care about these experiences except for friends and family and a few curious professional folks looking for a behind the scenes account of what it's like to be a showrunner? Then I got a job that would impact me like no other job ever has. Darren and I were hired to take over the showrunning duties of a television show called SHADOWHUNTERS, a young adult, science fiction-fantasy drama entering its second season.

The gig didn't feel life-altering at the time. It felt overwhelming and challenging in the best way. And then I met the fandom - first on Twitter, then in person at the various Comic-Cons - and I quickly realized how much this show and book series meant to so many people around the world. Many of these book readers who had now turned into show viewers felt alone until these characters, created by Cassandra Clare, entered their lives. People who always felt like they were on the outside looking in, who always felt weird and different compared to everyone else in the world, were inspired by the books and the show to let their freak flag fly and not worry what others think.

They are a fiercely loyal and dedicated bunch. They vote online until their fingers are blistered in order to bestow award after award on the show. They're also protective. Hell hath no fury if you damage one of their beloved characters. They are brimming with creative energy - artists, musicians, editors, writers - and the desire to spread love and acceptance everywhere and anyway they can. Their campaign to save the show included donating a tremendous amount of their time and money in the name of #saveshadowhunters to cause positive change in this complicated world, and in so doing have inspired me to write this book and donate all its proceeds to *The Trevor Project* and *Mental Health America* in the name of #shadowhunterslegacy. Thank you for watching. Thank you for reading.

# PROLOGUE

*August 3, 2018*

*Toronto*

*1:45am*

Numb with adrenaline and exhaustion, I stared bleary-eyed at the video monitor where last minute hair and make-up touches were being applied to Kat McNamara. She'd been crying for hours by now, her eyes red and puffy, mascara running amok. Brian Hui, the head of the make-up department in season three and a bright light of creativity and positivity, was doing his best to help. But the tears wouldn't stop. Kat was a committed actor who was locked into her character, and her character was in deep pain. In the finale scenes that were shot today, Clary Fairchild, the art student turned shadowhunter, was about to lose all of her memories and had to subtextually say goodbye to three people dear and near to her heart. Her best friend Simon; her Aunt-like maternal figure Maryse; and of course, the love of her life, Jace. These three scenes took place at a wedding reception where the entire cast was present, including many actors from seasons past. It was a grand reunion filled with warm nostalgia. A special day that brought back many familiar faces and sweet memories.

We had designed the day to shoot the script in order of how it would appear in the final cut, a rare occurrence given the various constraints on production. This was important so we could try to preserve Kat's emotional energy and allow it to build organically through what was sure to be a grueling and devastatingly emotional day. And now we were in the final stretch. And Kat couldn't stop crying. Not only because the script called for it; today was also the last day of production on the show she had been shooting for the last four years. Three seasons. Fifty-five episodes. Her entire adult life. And it would all be over after this one last shot.

I was watching the video monitor on the Institute operations set, which had been turned into a wedding chapel for Alec and Magnus' wedding ceremony earlier in the week by the phenomenal art department. The flowers and decorations were still everywhere. Today it was set up as "video village", where the director and various crew members could watch the three monitors hooked up to the three cameras on set. Usually the director, cinematographer, script supervisor and hair and make-up crew huddle around the monitors, but tonight hundreds of people stood behind me. The entire crew had showed up. Even many who weren't working.

Isaiah Mustafa, who was shooting IT CHAPTER TWO in Toronto, was there with his wife Lisa. Dominic Sherwood's father had travelled from England and was beaming with pride. Chris Hatcher, the extraordinary line producer in charge of the budget and logistics, was there with the entire production office staff. Brian Lenard, our amazing network executive, had tears in his eyes. Phillipe Thibaut, the trusted VFX guru of Shadowhunters who had been by my side every day of the finale shoot, sat in a chair with his laptop shockingly closed, staring into nothingness through a fog of bittersweet shock. They were there to celebrate the end, and they were getting thirsty. A cart full of champagne bottles was parked nearby, seemingly beckoning for people to pop them open. But no one dared take a sip before the shot was completed and the director yelled "cut", and that was me. The pressure of having these hundreds of people waiting on me to get the party started was too much so I headed to the set, to watch the shot on the tiny monitor by the camera, to slip inside my own space for this one last gasp.

As I turned to step out, I thought I was stricken with double vision. There were two Madzie's wearing identical red dresses, playing together. This was the actress Ariana Williams and her body double, who was there in case we had to go over the allotted time we had to shoot a young child. But it wouldn't be necessary today. The last shot would be Clary walking away from Jace and the rest of the reception, where the rest of the cast were slow dancing to Emmit Fenn's "1995" blasting over the speakers on set (which I'm listening to as I write this). For the wedding and reception, I had identified the songs early on knowing that I wanted to play them on set as we shot the scenes to help the actors find their groove. This particular song made me cry the first time I heard it in my hotel room in Toronto. Our music supervisor, the sonic superstar aka Lindsay Wolfington, had a habit of picking the perfect song for every single scene, and these songs were simply perfect. Earlier in the day, as Dom and Kat slow danced to this song (a scene I referred to as the "every single cell in my body" scene), I had steady tears in my eyes, as did Dom's Dad sitting a few rows behind me.

For the last shot there would only be one camera, "A" camera, operated masterfully by Drew Potter, who had been on show since season one. The camera would be close to the ground on dolly tracks, moving back while Clary walked toward us. I walked into the reception, which was now darkened for this last moody moment. The cast was paired off for the last dance -- Matt and Harry, Alberto and Emeraude, Nicola and little Jack, Sydney and Jackie, Lorenzo and Underhill, Kat and Dom. I approached Kat, who was barely hanging on, the emotion overpowering her. I asked if she was ready for this. The last moment. She nodded. Holding myself together, I muttered "let's do this" and headed back to the monitor. Siluck Sayanasy, the first assistant director on this shoot who began in season one and directed two terrific episodes of his own in season three, quieted everyone down. Drew lined up his camera. I adjusted my headphones and yelled "action". Kat began her walk-away, the tears streaming down her face. Dom whispered under his breath, "I love you, too". Kat continued her tragic walk, the camera gently gliding backwards until she turned and left frame. I took a deep breath and the word softly spilled out of my mouth. "Cut".

For most of the people in the building, the journey was over. The show was done. It would be their last day working on this special show. The sets would be dismantled and destroyed. The props and wardrobe would be (shamelessly and prematurely) sold. I would be tasked with editing my director's cut back in Los Angeles, then working with my writing and producing partner Darren Swimmer on a network cut, on the visual effects, the sound mix, and the color -- just like we'd done on the previous forty episodes of Shadowhunters. As the cast and crew hurried to pour champagne and prepare for the final toast, l realized how truly blessed I was to be a part of something so special. My journey into the shadow world began in such a bizarre, surreal way, it was only fitting it would end at a wedding with a glass of champagne in my hand.

# DOOR INTO THE DARK

*August 2, 2016*
*Los Angeles*
*5:00pm*

The phone call came on a late, sun-drenched Tuesday afternoon. I was at my mother's house, visiting with relatives from out of town, when my phone rang and flashed the caller ID of a network executive, Jenn Gerstenblatt, who we were working with on a show called GUILT. It was a neo-noir crime thriller shot in London created by two fantastic writers and people, Kathryn Price and Nichole Millard. We were in post-production and I assumed the phone call was about the last cut we had turned in. The assistant called Darren as well, and soon Jenn came on the line asking us a single question that would end up turning our lives upside down: "Have you guys ever seen the show Shadowhunters?"

We had not. She explained season two was beginning production on Monday and they were making a change at the showrunner position. She urged us to watch the show as soon as possible and get back to her tomorrow morning. That night, as soon as I came home, I watched the pilot. My first reaction was that the show felt very young. The lighting was so bright, the props, including the light saber swords, looked very cheesy, and the pace was frantic. Every scene moved by at rapid speed, with more of an emphasis on plot than emotion. But the cast...

my God, the cast was fantastic. Every single one of them was so charismatic. My wife Tali came in and peered at the screen and was blown away by their beauty. After watching a few more episodes, I picked up the book and read a chapter, and I realized this adaptation felt different than the books. The books were darker in tone, and had more yearning and sturm and drang, the operatic emotion I loved deeply embedded in its DNA. I was more than intrigued.

The following day Darren and I called Jenn and said we were open to the adventure but there were changes we wanted to make. Our first issue was the visual style. The executive assured us that they felt the same way and had hired a new producer director for season two, a gentleman by the name of Matt Hastings. This was great news. We met Matt when we were consulting producers in the show ALPHAS for ten weeks in 2012. He was a very gifted director with a strong visual style, and we knew the show was in good hands. When we mentioned our issues with pacing and storytelling, Jenn said they were on the same page and would support us every step of the way. No meeting was necessary. The network wanted us to run the show. I was shocked. This never happened to us. When Darren and I get offered jobs, we normally have to take at least one, often two, sometimes three meetings where we pitch our ideas and vision for the show to various executives. But there was no time in this situation. They needed us desperately and trusted that we could deliver a show they'd be proud of, which was extremely flattering and highly intimidating. We were ready to hammer out a deal to come aboard.

Jenn said once there was a deal, they would send us all the material that had already been generated. At that point there were three finished scripts and an episode outline for 204. So while our agent and attorney negotiated our deal, we read more of the book and prepared ourselves for what was sure to be one hell of a ride. On Friday our agent and lawyer called to say the deal was close and we could start that Monday morning. But the network still didn't send the material until our deal was officially closed on Sunday evening. When the scripts and outlines flooded my email inbox, I knew if I read now there would be no way I would be able to sleep. My mind would be racing with thoughts about the stories.

So instead, I opened up a bottle of wine and sat down to watch a baseball game. The following morning I woke up at 5 AM to read the first two scripts. We had a lot of work to do.

# DAY ONE

Early Monday morning Darren and I drove into the Shadowhunters office together. We used to carpool when we began our career in television, but these days it was a rare occurrence when we drove into work together. Our commutes had become our "alone time" -- our chance to make personal calls, listen to music or talk radio, and spend time in our own heads. I drove as we navigated our way into the bowels of Hollywood, driving up Vine, making a right turn onto Delongpre, and stopping outside of a series of ramshackle craftsman homes shielded behind a rusted security gate. This was the Shadowhunters Writers offices and post-production facility? Apparently it was, because outside stood a young woman, stylishly dressed, with a big smile on her face. "Are you guys Todd and Darren?" She introduced herself as Zoe Broad, the former showrunner's assistant and our initial guide into the shadow world. And what a guide she was. Zoe was smart and knew everything about the show. She was instrumental in getting us up on our feet and filling us in on so many details we needed to know.

Zoe used her security key card to open the gate and we drove into the pock-marked parking lot between the series of bungalows that had apparently all been turned into offices for writers or editors. How bizarre. It was early, around 9

AM, so there was no one around (television writers usually begin their day at 10 AM). The three of us were the only ones there, the hot, bright Hollywood sun blinding as Zoe led us toward a dilapidated, two-story Bungalow. On the first floor was a writer's room inside the kitchen. I'd never seen anything like it. There was a refrigerator and a toaster oven and a series of snacks on the table and in the middle of the room was a large conference table surrounded by chairs, with several poles coming down from the ceiling to the floor as if to hold the place together. She then let us up a rickety flight of stairs where there were four tiny offices and a bathroom. We peeked into the largest of the four offices, which wasn't large at all, and realized this would be where we would be spending most of our days and many of our nights during the next year.

We decided to reach out to the cast as soon as possible, one by one over the phone, to introduce ourselves. We knew we would meet them in person when we flew up to Toronto later in the week, but it was important for us to connect with them personally and let them know how supportive and excited we were and that their show wasn't about to crumble. We also wanted them to know that getting rewritten pages the night before shooting was not the norm. While some television shows make it a practice of writing scenes down to the wire and delivering pages the night before, with little time for the actors to absorb the material, it wasn't our process. After this initial episode, they would always have a locked script before the episode went to camera to give them as much time to prepare as possible. We understood many of them were filming that day so our connection would be sporadic throughout the afternoon, so we began our calls at the top of the call sheet.

Kat McNamera was warm and welcoming, and very interested to hear our thoughts on the show. We immediately understood how protective she was of Clary and promised we would treat her with great care. At 19, she already felt like a total pro. It was strange to hear Dom Sherwood with an American accent when we knew he was British. He told us that when he was on set, he always maintained his American accent, which I thought was professional and cool. Alberto Rosende told us he used to watch Smallville when he was young with his friends and was

13

so excited to be working with us. We told him how excited we were to be working with such a talented actor. It turned out that Isaiah Mustafa was friends with Michael Rosenbaum, the amazing actor who played Lex Luthor on Smallville. Apparently Michael had nice things to say about us and Isaiah seemed excited to work with us. We told him that we thought

Luke had a lot of comic potential and we wanted to lean into humor whenever we could. Isaiah was down with that. Harry Shum Jr. was as nice as could be. I told him that my daughter was a huge Glee fan, and Mike Chang was one of her favorite characters. Her dream would come true when she was able to FaceTime with Harry at one of the many cast dinners we had in Toronto. Matt Daddario was kind and cordial but appeared a bit more guarded than the others. Matt was clearly intelligent and was excited that we wanted to make the show a bit more adult. He was also extremely protective of Alec, especially regarding his relationship with Magnus. We promised we would treat the relationship with great care and understood how much it meant to so many people throughout the world. We were so excited to write a relationship between an innocent, recently closeted gay man and an immortal bisexual warlock. It was brimming with possibilities and we couldn't wait to get started. Emeraude Toubia could not have been sweeter. She seemed like a total team player and promised to do whatever we needed from her. We told her that we wanted to make Izzy more cerebral. Her sexuality had been explored in season one and we now wanted to lean into her brains and the vulnerability behind her bad ass exterior. Isabelle Lightwood was so beautiful and flawless on the outside. We yearned to dig deeper into her psychology.

The network called to get our take on the material they sent over the night before. We were very honest and thought that the first episode needed a dialogue polish and the second episode needed to be rethought. Instead of having a heart attack, they were supportive and encouraged us to do whatever was needed. We explained that we would re-write the next day's work on this first episode without changing anything in terms of production. No new locations or complicated props. We called Matt Hastings, who was directing that first episode, and explained the situation. He was absolutely on board and grateful, excited by what we felt would be improvements. Matt is an extremely gifted director and experienced pro and could adapt to anything we threw his way.

It was now time to meet the writing staff. We knew there would be a lot of anxiety among the writers. They had been waiting a week for news of new leadership, and the previous showrunner had been battling with the network for the last few months over the material. So understandably they were particularly vulnerable. Plus, at this point no one knew if their job was secure. The great news was we had just learned that all the writers had "pay-or-play" deals, meaning they were guaranteed their salary for the rest of the season. Talk about the best icebreaker ever. What better way to begin our first conversation together by telling them all their jobs were secure?

Zoe let us down the rickety stairs and we stepped into the writer's room/kitchen, where we were greeted by a room full of smiling but battle-weary writers. As soon as we explained their salary was guaranteed, I could feel their anxiety rise up and float away. We went around the room and had each writer introduce and tell us about themselves, something we do every first day in our writer rooms. It was an opportunity for us to quickly get a handle on who these people were whom we would be spending the next eight months with making 20 episodes of television. In the ensuing week we would sit down with each of them individually in our office for a longer conversation. Luckily for us, they were all warm, friendly and smart people who could not have been nicer.

Taylor Mallory was the writer's assistant from season one who was in charge of transcribing and distilling all the ideas that were bantered about in the writer's room. She had read all of the Shadowhunters books as a teenager and was a true fan. Allison Rymer, a staff writer, was the script coordinator during season one. She was from Florida and sharp as Izzy's whip, full of ideas. Ally had an adorable, Maltese-Yorki dog named Carmela who came to work most days and sat on Ally's lap like the princess she was. Zac Hug, a mensch from the Midwest (Ohio), was another staff writer new to the show. He used to write trailers and other promotional clips, including a few for a show that we had worked on called DOMINION for SYFY. Zac had a great sense of humor with just the right amount of quirk. Pete Binswanger was a story editor who was on the writing staff in season one. Pete was from Philadelphia, a young, bright, lovable video gamer and movie geek. Pete was a wickedly talented writer and a very funny dude. He often brought his poodle mutt James, a sweet soul who looked perpetually stoned. Hollie Overton was a writer/producer who had worked with the previous showrunner and was also new to the show. She was a successful novelist from the heart of Texas with an abundance of strength and emotional power both in her work and in her person, as well as a wonderful sense of humor. Hollie had her own fabulous rescue Chihuahua-mix named Stevie. Shireen Razack was a writer/producer from season one and also the partner of the uber talented Anupam Nigam, a writer we had worked with for three seasons on SyFy's DEFIANCE. Jamie Gorenberg, the Co-Executive Producer, was brought on in season two. A seasoned veteran with a long list of credits in both comedy and drama, Jamie was new to genre television and eager to learn. Talented and hyper-analytical, she was currently in charge of the writer's room because the previous showrunner's second in command, Executive Producer Michael Reisz, was currently on set in Toronto, producing the season two premiere he had written. Michael had been running things after the previous showrunner left and had done an amazing job keeping the wheels from falling off the cart during that chaotic few days before we came aboard. We would meet Michael when we flew up to Toronto the following week.

Once we finished our introductions, we began to convey the changes we wanted to make to the show. First off, we wanted to slow down the pace and create scenes with fewer characters, where we would have the room to lean into the emotional core of each scene rather than focus on plot. Those were our favorite moments in season one. Our motto moving forward was less missions, more emotion. We longed to get deeper into the heads of these awesome characters like the books do and knew the actors would want the same thing and rise to the occasion. Our least favorite scenes in season one were when there were six or seven characters in a scene talking about the mission at hand. We knew those scenes were necessary at times, but we wanted to reduce them as much as we could. We also wanted to create more of a binge-worthy momentum by ending every show with a scene we described as a "holy shit moment" that made you have to watch the next episode. And the more of those scenes in the final act the better.

We also realized there were simply too many characters in the show. It was impossible to properly service all these souls, as wonderful as they all were. So we went about the difficult task of trying to reduce the number of characters we would be focusing on. We knew this was a minefield because the fandom was so passionate and all these characters were worshipped. But at the end of the day we had to trust our instincts, as controversial as they might be. We desperately needed the writers to educate us about the deep mythology of the shadow world. It all felt overwhelming to quickly comprehend. We had just begun to dissect book one and knew that given our workload, it would take us awhile to get through the series. So the writing staff patiently filled us in and reminded us again and again what rune did what.

Because episode 202 would begin prep the following day, that was our priority in the writer's room. I had read the script that morning and loved Magnus and Simon going to India. Valentine was kidnapping people on a subway train, which was cool but felt random and very difficult to produce given our budget constraints. We zeroed in on the idea of Valentine abducting fighters in martial arts and boxing gyms, environments we could quickly produce well and a platform that would give Izzy a chance to kick some serious ass. We introduced the idea of Clary wanting to return to her old life as an art student. It was an opportunity to humanize Clary and remind the audience that at her core, she's just like one of us. The idea of Clary getting kidnapped by Dot and brought back to Valentine's ship was also new and exciting, and we loved the concept of Clary being crafty and trying to manipulate this woman she's known her entire life to break Dot out of Valentine's mind control.

Once we had a rough idea of this new basic concept, we set up a call that evening at 6pm to pitch to the network, Constantin Film (who owned the rights to the book and funded season one) and the production team in Toronto. It would be over a speaker phone in the writer's room, with yours truly delivering the play by play. Exciting to say the least. The good news was the director of the episode, Andy Wolk, was someone we had worked with before on Defiance. Andy had directed everything from The Sopranos to Ugly Betty, and his work on Defiance blew us away. He was also a sweet human being who took the time to go to lunch with me and give me pointers before I directed my first episode for Defiance. I knew we were in good hands with an experienced filmmaker who would be able to adapt deftly to a brand-new script that would be evolving daily.

While the writers continued to "break the story" (break means create -- weird, right?), Darren and I went upstairs to our cramped office, closed the door, and I started to kind of freak out. This was an insane situation. We had been up against the wall numerous times on many different shows, but this was different. The amount of work that needed to be done in such a short period of time was literally overwhelming us. We sat at our facing desks and made a pledge to ourselves. We would only focus on the next task right in front of us instead of letting our racing thoughts take us to the millions of other things that needed to be done after that. It would be the best way to tackle the workflow and control my anxiety in those first weeks.

First thing up was connecting with Michael Reisz immediately. Michael was an executive producer and the leader of the writer's room. He was instrumental in the success of season 1, in particularly the relationship between Magnus, a centuries-old, bisexual Asian warlock, and Alec, a 22-year-old white shadowhunter not yet out of the closet. The episode "Malec", which Michael penned, was our favorite of season one. He had worked for Ed Decter on many shows as Ed's second in command, so I anticipated it could be a difficult conversation, which I was used to at this point in my career but never something I looked forward to. It would be perfectly understandable for Michael to be cold toward us, but when we connected over the phone, he could not have been warmer and more welcoming. He pledged to do whatever we needed from him to make the show what we wanted it to be. He completely understood us rewriting his script but asked if we could leave the Malec scenes alone. And we gladly said yes.

They were fantastic scenes, and the last thing we wanted to do was mess up the things that worked. We told Michael we were coming up to Canada the following week and looked forward to meeting him in person.

Usually when Darren and I write or rewrite an episode of television, we split up scenes and then swap them to tweak each other's work. But Shadowhunters was brand new to us and we wanted to make sure we were on the same wavelength when it came to tone and voices. We started in on the scenes in 201 aka "This Guilty Blood" that would be shooting the next day: Jace and Maria-the-Vampire facing off in the pizza parlor at the end of the show, and Valentine encouraging Jace to kill her. We added dialogue to the scene of Clary and Simon running through the park. It all felt good and we were getting into our groove. When we write, it is very easy and quite common to completely lose track of time. That's why we have an assistant who peeks their head in to alert us to the next task ahead. Zoe told us the call with the network was in an hour. We had planned to spend time in the writer's room before the call to hear the new ideas and sculpt the pitch.

The writers were brimming with smart thoughts and their enthusiasm was infectious. It seemed that the excitement of a new beginning had energized the writer's room, as well as the knowledge that their jobs were safe and their new bosses weren't horrible human beings. We quickly settled on the basic structure that you see in the episode and dialed in for the call. Throughout our career, Darren and I have contributed equally to the work, but I was the one who verbally pitched our ideas. Whether it's an original movie or pilot idea, or simply an episode of a show, I always get a pit in my stomach before I start. Today was no different. The stakes were high. This was the first time the people that hired us would hear our ideas for the show, told through the lens of episode 202. It was also the first time we would meet Robert Kulzer and Margo Klewans from Constantin Film, who were both up in Toronto with Jenn Gerstenblatt to be on set for the first few days of filming on episode 2. Matt Hastings was also listening in with them on his lunch break from directing episode 201, as well as Brian Lenard and Kirsten Creamer, the network executives in L.A, and Mary Viola, McG's partner and an executive producer. I pitched the episode with the energy and passion I felt for the material, and the response was positive. We ordered dinner and began working on a rough outline with the staff. Darren and I started to sputter out in a fog of exhaustion around eight, telling the staff not to stay too late. We would see them in the morning.

# BY THE LIGHT OF DAWN

We awoke to the rough outline in our email, sent at 2:30am. We were impressed with the turnaround but worried that the staff was pushing themselves too hard. When we all assembled in the room that morning, we praised them for the amazing document and their tireless work ethic but warned them of burning themselves out. It would be a marathon not a sprint. Because we needed a script as soon as humanly possible, each member of the staff would write an act of the script so we would be able to have a "completed" script within twenty-four hours. This process, which we like to call "barn-raising", has become increasingly common on writing staffs for many successful television shows. Darren and I have participated in this process before as writers on staff, and found it produces diminishing returns and wears down writers as they race to complete pages they know have to be rewritten to fit together. Our process involves one writer or writing team penning a first draft, then writing another draft based on our notes. Barn-raising was only used in an emergency when time was of the essence, and this happened to be one of those times. Shireen was a great writer who wrote a solid draft, but it was based on another vision of the show, and as a total professional, she completely understood the need for a good old barn raise. It would also give me and Darren an opportunity to read each writer's work and get to know their style. We told the staff to go home or wherever they felt comfortable writing and email us their pages by ten am the following day.

We hurried up the shambling steps to our office and turned on our computer monitors, remembering to focus on the priority at that moment, which was now the pages for tomorrow's work. The dailies from 201 had arrived and Darren and I could not wait to see the new look. Unfortunately, the blinding August sunlight was pouring in through the broken mini-blinds hanging over an unusually large amount of windows for such a small office. The glare was crazy. Zoe was on it. The following day we would have black-out curtains that could not only block out the sun but the exterior world to create our own shadow world -- much like Darren's parent's garage and our recording studio experiences years ago. Once we found the right angle, we watched in awe. The show looked fantastic. It was a complete overhaul from season one. Matt Hastings and his creative team had orchestrated a stunning visual makeover. It felt so much more cinematic, more frightening, more adult. We wanted to watch more but Zoe informed us the concept meeting for episode 202 was about to begin.

The pre-production of every episode of television begins with a concept meeting, where the showrunner, the writer of that episode, the director, and the various production department heads go over the script scene by scene. Usually led by the first assistant director, the director can throw out any ideas they have and the department heads can understand their vision and flag any potential problems. This meeting would be unique for many reasons. First off, the script they were holding was no longer the script that would be shot. For many shows this is not uncommon, but for Darren and I it never happened. We made it a priority to always stay ahead of production so we could have a super strong, tight script on the first day of prep. Today we had a very rough beat sheet with many holes to be filled, so it would be necessary to pitch the show. It was also the first time we would be meeting the department heads that we would be working with on the next twenty episodes, and it had to be done over Skype, which is always strange no matter how you slice it.

We sat on our tiny couch with Shireen and faced a computer monitor, where we squinted through the glare at a long conference table filled with talented people. The first person we recognized was the maestro Matt Hastings, the dapper producer/director in his jacket and tie, Red Sox cap firmly in place, smile wide. We immediately greeted each other and told him and everyone in that room how blown away we were by the dailies and the entire look of the show. They all were absolutely killing it. Of course it was music to their ears and immediately broke the awkwardness and weirdness of the arrival of "the new boss." For all they knew we could have been total assholes. There are a few of them in Hollywood. The other person we recognized was my friend Andy Wolk, who took in the unknown of this upcoming journey with ease. Thank God a total pro was directing this. We met Greg Copeland, the kind, jovial line producer in charge of the budget and logistics. The brilliant and sweet Doug McCullough led the art department. Darren McGuire, a swirling ball of talent and infectious energy, was in charge of stunts. David Herrington, a British Gentlemen, was the cinematographer for the even numbered episodes. Always smiling, rock and roll Mike McMurray, the other cinematographer, was shooting 201 with Matt but was sitting in as well to meet us. The costume designer, Shelley Mansell, was a talent to behold who dug into the script and managed to dress each character in the perfect wardrobe for what the scene needed. Anthony "Tony Smokes" Germinario was the prop master and one of the best in the business. Over the phone our Toronto casting agent, Lisa Parasyn, was listening in. We had worked with Lisa previously on DEFIANCE, and it was good to hear her familiar, friendly voice. Tommy Summers, the producer in charge post-production we had yet to meet, was conferenced in from the bungalow next door to us.

After filling them all in on the new show, we sensed their relief. They were thrilled that we were giving up the idea of shooting on a subway train and excited by the fight club direction. Stunt coordinator Darren McGuire was obviously pumped, as was the art department and line producer who recognized the cost savings by design and shooting the fight club at our studio. John Rakich, the creative, resourceful location coordinator, vowed to find a mansion that could feel like it was somewhere in India. The boat stuff was manageable because we already had the location. We were in good shape. We told them they would get a work in progress draft tomorrow evening.

Our post-production team was housed in an adjacent bungalow within this bizarre gated block in the thick of Hollywood, and Darren and I decided it was time to pay them a visit and introduce ourselves. Post-production is important on every show, but for a science fiction/fantasy show overflowing with visual effects, it was vital and could often make or break an episode. While season one had some cool visual effects from time to time, we thought it was a real weak spot and had to be improved. Luckily Matt Hastings felt the same way and was already working closely with the vfx team to improve upon what had already been created. We met Geoff Leavitt, the vfx producer with a big fat heart who had coincidentally graduated from Hamilton High School, the same school Darren and I went to. We immediately bonded and were excited to see rough versions of the new Magnus magic. The portals felt greatly improved, as did his cat eyes. The purple hues that rubbed us the wrong way were replaced by a cool fiery orange hue. We learned that the visual effects were farmed out to different companies who specialized in different things, instead of one company overseeing the entire account, which was what we were used to.

We met the producer in charge of post-production, Tommy Summers, a warm-hearted dude full of energy who cut his teeth on successful Disney Channel movies, including HIGH SCHOOL MUSICAL, and was coming off SWITCHED AT BIRTH, a successful Freeform drama that had been recently cancelled. Musicians ourselves, we immediately recognized the spirit of a drummer, which Tommy confirmed. He led us down the dark narrow hall to one of the three editing bays. A show of this size usually has three editors, but only one was currently working at the moment. Pete Gvodas was hugely talented and normally worked on pilots and movies as opposed to episodic television. He too was enthusiastic about the dailies and told us he loved the show and wanted to work on the series. Knowing we had two other seasoned editors, Randy Bricker from season one and the wunderkind Nate Easterling who Matt had hired after working with him on THE ORIGINALS, made us feel confident things in post were under control.

Now that our involvement had been announced in the press, Zoe suggested we reach out to the fans on Twitter. I had never been a big Twitter user. I opened an account when we did the reboot of MELROSE PLACE in 2009 and then used it sporadically during my days on other television shows. It was a great way to interact with fans, but there weren't too many fans to interact with on those shows. In fact, when we were live tweeting with Guilt, I would notice that any post from the official Shadowhunters account would generate hundreds if not thousands of likes. So I changed my profile page and tweeted out a post recognizing the talented people that came before me who helped make the show. Thus began my entry into the shadowhunters Twitterverse, a community of diehard fans, most of whom were warm and welcoming. I immediately recognized how important the show was to so many people. It was inspiring and intimidating at the same time.

Pages for the following day's work were the next priority. We dove into the belly of Valentine's ship with Jace and Clary, and the scene in the galley where Valentine makes Jace spaghetti. It was a strong scene in the shooting script, so we were cautious not to mess it all up with our tweaks. Fortunately, the network liked the work we did the previous day, so there was no time to second guess ourselves at this point. We had to trust our instincts and move forward. We finished the pages and sent them off to the script coordinator to be proofread then distributed to the entire crew and cast in Toronto, as well as the executives and writing and post staff here in L.A. The job requires a keen eye for bad spelling and typos and off the hook organizational skills, abilities Darren and I sorely lack. A bad coordinator can screw things up good. But we felt completely at ease with Joey Elkins, a seasoned pro and a gifted writer and visual artist. We trusted him to correct our errors and headed home to read the script for the following episode, 203, and as much of the books as I could while my eyes remained open.

The compiled script came in the following morning, and while a bit jagged and uneven due to the six acts written by six different writers, the story seemed to track and there were some great moments throughout. The staff was extremely talented, and they knew the show well. But they had only read the five or six scenes we had rewritten in episode 201. It was too soon for them to understand our sensibility and the new, more emotional tone we wanted to set. We would now do a pass on the script while Shireen covered the episode's prep meetings over the phone with each of the department heads. Before we disappeared upstairs, we thanked everyone for the great work they turned around in such a short period of time and spoke in broad brush strokes about the next episode.

The existing script by Pete Binswanger was in good shape but the story flowed from 202 which had now been significantly retooled. There would still be wolves. Maia Roberts, one of my favorite characters from the books, was being introduced. This would be the first character Darren and I would be in charge of bringing to the screen. The other seven leads had been expertly cast by Ed Decter, who developed the books for television and was the showrunner in season one and the prep of season two. We'd never met Ed but heard great things about him from the entire cast and crew. The character of Maia was beloved by fans, and we knew we had to get it right. We also knew we wanted to introduce Hunter's Moon, the bar where downworlders, humans and shadowhunters could all hang out. Allison Rymer came up with the idea of Maia being a bartender. The room was revving up its engines. The plotlines were all clear and simple. Jace has to get to Alec to save his parabatai while being hunted by the Clave and the Wolves. Magnus has to heal Alec before he was thrown out of the Institute. Torn between her allegiance to her old life and the shadow world, Clary has to find Jace and help Simon, who has to find his mom before her drunken binge gets her into trouble. The stories felt right.

We left to go write the sides for the upcoming Maia auditions. Sides are scenes that are specifically used to audition a character. Sometimes they are plucked from an existing script, but in many cases they're uniquely crafted to showcase an auditioning actor's range of emotions. Once in our office, we began to write. But as is the nature of the job of a showrunner, especially when one's first day on the job is the first day of production on season two, you cannot write for more than fourteen uninterrupted minutes. Today it was a very important phone call.

It was our priority to sit down or speak with every person who has been intricately involved with the show since its inception, the first being the person who created it all. Cassandra Clare was the author behind a book empire that has sold over 32 million copies. One of her many book series, The Mortal Instruments comprises six of the books that Constantin and Freeform owned and upon which Shadowhunters was based on. Since we began our career in television, it was always important to us that the creators of the material/showrunners we were writing for were happy with our work. It is the only way to succeed as a television writer. We knew Cassie, like the network, wasn't thrilled with season one, and we were eager to express our new vision for the show which would hopefully more fully capture the vibe of the powerful emotional moments in the books. We were also terrified about how she was going to react to the first huge bombshell we would drop on the canon she had so elegantly created.

Cassie was writing in the Caribbean when we connected over the phone, and she could not have been warmer and more friendly. She was a fan of Smallville, which she recognized was also an adaptation of beloved canon. When she heard we wanted to lean more into the emotionality that she captured in the pages in her books, she was thrilled. Now it was time to drop the bombshell. There were too many supporting characters on the show. If we wanted to spend the time to dig deeper into our seven lead characters, those supporting characters would have to be trimmed. Cassie understood and agreed wholeheartedly. Now was the hard part. We explained that Clary's hero's journey felt too safe and emotionally easy with her mother by her side. Maxim Roy is a fine actress but her presence on the show was impeding Clary's growth. We wanted to shake things up for Clary in a profound way and throw her into the deep end of life's swimming pool. We wanted her to be alone in a world of shadows, a world that her mom could no longer explain to her. We wanted to kill Jocelyn. There was a gasp. Then silence… then the words we longed to hear. She thought it was a good idea. She understood

27

that the show was a different beast than the books and would veer in other directions from time to time. Darren and I vowed to treat her material with great respect and told her we looked forward to meeting her in person at New York Comic-Con in October.

Constantin Film owned the rights to the books. They had produced a movie based on the books in 2012, and years later a bright, forward-thinking executive at the company, Margo Klewans, suggested making it into a television show to her boss Robert Kulzer. The company hired Ed Decter to write a pilot and sold the show to Freeform for domestic broadcast and Netflix for the rest of the world, with the talented director McG shooting the first episode and executive producing the series with his producing partner Mary Viola. They had produced thirteen episodes that earned them another season, no easy feat. We would meet Robert and Margo in Canada next week, but McG and Mary Viola were in L.A., so we immediately arranged a sit down. I've been a big fan of McG's since the original CHARLIE'S ANGELS movie, one of the best film adaptations of a television show in my humble opinion, and I was excited to meet him. The most memorable moments of my career are the times I get to meet creative people whose work I truly admire. I will always geek out when I meet someone I am in awe of, but I always manage to get it together and pretend I'm cool when I walk into the meeting. We met McG in the morning at a cafe across from his office on Sunset Boulevard. He could not have been more welcoming. Over his green kale smoothie, he filled us in on his experience with the various actors and crew and told us he was here whenever we needed him. If we wanted him to fly up to Toronto tomorrow, he'd do it. He loved this show and wanted it to succeed, and his unbridled enthusiasm lifted us up and made us smile. A legend like McG was in our corner.

Mary Viola was also an executive producer who was intimately involved in the show and had just been in Toronto. We met Mary for lunch at Cheebos in Hollywood and instantly connected. She was extremely supportive and asked if there was anything she could do. When we told her we felt like we were getting a handle and looked forward to hearing her notes on things, we could feel the relief sweeping over. Mary had been embroiled in a tense situation the past few months in the middle of the madness, running interference, and now she could just be creative. We too left that lunch feeling relieved. When you start a new project, you never know what personalities lurk behind the names, and knowing how awesome and reasonable Mary was made us feel good.

The script for 202 was our task at hand, interruptions and all. Production and the network beckoned for a draft, but we wanted to give them something as solid as possible. This would be the script for the first episode under our watch. While we would get credit on 201, all we did to the script were dialogue tweaks. But this script, whether it worked or not, was on us. Ignoring the outside world and internal pressure, we plowed through, scene after scene, trying to interject as much emotion as we could without getting too maudlin. The scene in Clary's bedroom with Izzy trying to cheer Clary up remains one of my favorites. I love Simon and the snake. Valentine on the ship with his son and daughter is awesome. As we blocked out the sun with our new black-out curtains and cranked Bon Iver, it didn't feel like work. It felt like we were geeked out teenagers playing music in Darren's parents' garage.

Before we knew it Friday was upon us and we had to deliver a draft whether we were ready or not. We were travelling to Toronto on Monday and they would be prepping while we were flying. We hit send and went down to the writer's room, where we heard the new ideas taking shape for 203. I suggested doing flashbacks of little Jace and Alec to illustrate how their parabatai bond came to be. I've always loved flashbacks, especially when we get to see children versions of the adults. We also talked about redeeming Jocelyn by having her save Jace at the hospital. We wanted the audience on her side before her tragic demise now planned for the following episode. Once we felt like there was enough there, we asked the room to put together a beat sheet (a slimmed down version of an outline that doesn't get into story details but just conveys the gist of each scene) that we could send to the network as opposed to a verbal pitch since we would be in Toronto the following week. This was a weekend when everyone could take a bit of a breather, except for me and Darren who still had five books to read. I told

Darren I'd run point with Shireen on publishing 202 and see him at the airport Monday morning.

That weekend a close friend of mine was turning fifty and invited my wife and I up to Ojai to celebrate. My wife had left earlier, knowing I couldn't get there until late. As I drove up the dark, winding roads, my phone rang. It was Shireen, who had some suggested tweaks to the script. It had always been our process to send our rewrite to the original writer to make sure it tracks and to correct any inconsistencies. She had smart suggestions which we executed, and then the question of a title arose. Because Clary was kidnapped through the portal, I suggested "In Through The Out Door", the title of an old Led Zeppelin song that felt oddly appropriate. Shireen said they usually titled shows after chapters in the books. I understood, but was there something as cool and fitting as "In Through the Out Door?" She brought up "A Door Into the Dark" and that was that. It was a perfect title and perfect metaphor for what we were about to go through.

# NORTH

The black town car sat idling outside of my house as I frantically searched for my missing passport, a process I was fairly used to. It's never where it should be but I always find it in the end. I dragged my rolling carry-on suitcase outside, squinting into the sunlight. The suit-clad driver opened the door for me and took my bag to place it in the trunk. This was not a life I was accustomed to, and I never took the perk for granted. Travelling business class was required by the union whenever writers and directors needed to travel a certain amount of distance for work, and it was always a real treat, especially when you had work to do on the plane. My entry into first class travel was on Smallville, only a two-hour flight from Los Angeles to Vancouver. That show was also my introduction to the positive, progressive, awesome culture of Canada. Whether it was Vancouver or Toronto, the various people I've met over the years have always been so warm and kind.

I met Darren in the first-class lounge, another sweet perk. We soon met Shireen, who would be gone for the next two weeks for the rest of prep and the duration of the shoot. On Shadowhunters and all of their shows, the network liked to have a writer on set. Darren and I would only be here a few days, returning

Thursday morning after the table read on Wednesday. Most shows conduct table reads, where the cast gathers to read the script and the writers and network listen to see if there are any last-minute changes they want to make before it goes to camera. This visit would be more about meeting each of the cast members and department heads in person, but being there for the table read was a nice bonus.

Getting away for the weekend had been a nice respite, only interrupted by a few emails from The Powers That Be, who were worried that the dailies were visually too dark. I only had my iPad to watch them on, but I assured them that they could be corrected in color-timing, a process that was done on all episodes where we could tweak the colors and contrast. One of Matt Hastings first visual priorities was to darken the show and create more shadows, which we were totally on board with. But sometimes it was too dark even for me and Darren. We liked to see the light in the actor's eyes at all times, especially given how beautiful and expressive their eyes were. In subsequent episodes the cinematographers corrected, and the darkness gradually grew a bit lighter.

On the plane I read the outline for 204, which I quickly recognized had to be completely scratched. First off, it was based on the prior three shows which had now been significantly retooled. It was also the first episode after Jace was finally back in the Institute, and it was an opportunity to reset the show for the audience to experience a typical day in the life of a shadowhunter. If there was ever a time to lean into a bit of the procedural, it was here. I made some notes then dug into the books. And maybe ordered a glass of wine or three.

Once we landed and escaped customs, we headed straight to the studio, the town car replaced by a production van. Cruising along a maze of freeways, we arrived in Mississauga, a suburb twenty minutes north of downtown Toronto. Five minutes along a road of nondescript homes and dentist offices, a beige cluster of buildings that resembled a depressing industrial park appeared on the right. You'd never expect that beyond those walls were the stages where Shadowhunters was brought to life -- where the actors were inside reading our words, and a crew of hundreds was waiting to meet us. As they say, the shit was getting real.

We were ushered into the offices by a P.A. (Production assistant:

awesome entry level job if you work for someone cool that gets you close to the action. Requires patience and humility while making coffee and ordering meals). With dark, wood panelled walls and wall to call carpeting, the production office looked like it had been transported here from 1972, now bustling and full of young, bright-eyed personnel. The big-hearted line producer, Greg Copeland, was there to greet us with a warm hug. His U.P.M. (unit production manager in charge of crunching numbers and logistics), Chris Hatcher, politely shook our hands. We were led into our office right off the main bullpen, Executive Producer/Showrunner proudly displayed on the door. We had a second to ourselves when a knock on the door revealed Matt Hastings, vibrating with the adrenaline of having just directed a scene. We exchanged big hugs, thrilled to see each other. He only had a few minutes before he had to get back to set, but he wanted to quickly fill us in on his ideas involving post-production, many that were already in motion.

Matt wanted to hire a second-unit crew in New York to shoot texture footage that we could interweave through the cuts to help establish that we were in New York City. In the books the reader really felt like they were there, which helped to ground the story, but in Season One the character of New York was pretty much absent. Matt, Darren and I wanted to bring it back in a big way, including adding visual effects shots of New York to many of the exterior locations that would be shot in Toronto. It wasn't cheap, but if we budgeted correctly, we could pick and choose the moments to open the show up. Regarding the music, Matt wanted to hire an old colleague of his, Trevor Morris, who was currently doing VIKINGS and had done THE TUDORS and ALPHAS with Matt. Darren knew and admired Trevor's work and was excited to talk to him.

Darren ran point on our work with composers and sound mixers. As a musician himself, Darren had a great ear and was full of ideas for sound design. A musician as well, Matt was going to set up that call the following day during his lunch and also give us a chance to speak with Lindsay Wolfington, the music supervisor from season one who we all felt did a great job. It turns out that back in the day, Lindsay was an assistant to the music supervisors who did Smallville.

Lindsay had come into her own on ONE TREE HILL and has impeccable taste, with the ability to pick just the right song for any scene.

While he had a short break from filming, Matt was eager to show us the new and improved sets that they just finished for season two. We excitedly followed him down a brightly lit corridor full of more offices, past crew members eyeing the new regime with curiosity. We smiled back and shook hands but had to keep up with Matt's quick walk. Time is of the essence when you're shooting. Another quick turn and he pushed open a thick, wooden door, leading us into the darkness of the sound stage. Our eyes slowly adjusted as we followed him into Magnus' bigger and better penthouse apartment, where painters were doing last minute touches on the work that would be done the following day. It was huge. We saw the boat basin, where Simon was going to be living, and the belly of the ship used in 201 and 202. Matt suggested this could be turned into The Hunter's Moon, a bar for downworlders from the book that we were eager to turn into a set for the show. The Jade Wolf was cool, but it was a werewolf hang out, and we were looking for a place where every character on the show could cross with one another and interact. We asked Matt if the set could be ready for 203. Like he would do throughout the duration of the run, Matt said of course. There wasn't any challenge he would shy away from, no matter how insurmountable it appeared.

The door creaked open and a young woman who looked remarkably like Taylor Swift appeared, telling Matt he was wanted back on the set. Matt introduced us to Amanda Row, his assistant for the time being and a wickedly talented filmmaker in her own right. She had directed second unit stuff for MINORITY REPORT and HEMLOCK GROVE, and Matt explained that he had hired her with the hope of her being able to direct an episode. It felt like a big risk to give a show to someone who's never directed an episode of TV before, but at the moment we simply shrugged and nodded. Matt had to get back to set. We followed through the darkness, through another thick, wooden door, into the adjacent sound stage where lights lit up an unseen set. I headed toward the light, feeling self-conscious as I felt the crew's curious stares. As Matt went to set up his shot, we peeked into the set of the Institute Operations Center, where Maryse was about to make her grand speech. The set was extraordinary. Bigger than before, it was filled with extras. The monitors flickered with cool data and imagery. I turned back into the darkness to see pretty much the entire cast clustered together waiting to be called onto set. Emeraude Toubia, Matt Daddario, Kat McNamara, Harry Shum and his fiancé Shelby, and Nick Sagar, who played Aldertree, all sat patiently on director chairs. Their charisma and star power shined through the darkness. They were all extremely warm and welcoming, and we told them we were excited to sit down with each of them to talk about our vision for the show and their characters moving forward. When Siluck arrived to usher them to set, we shook hands, exchanged hugs, and told them we'd see more of them in the next few days.

We couldn't stay and watch because our phones lit up with a text from Zoe in Los Angeles. The writer's room sent us the beat sheet for episode 203 that was scheduled to go into the network that evening. We went back to our office to quickly read. The beat sheet was in great shape. It would be an emotional episode but it would also be full of drive and suspense, and a bar fight between Jace and Maia that would be absolutely awesome. One thing I loved about Shadowhunters was that the women all kicked ass. They didn't need to be coddled or taken care of by men. They were fine by themselves, and Maia was proof of that. We told Jamie Gorenberg, who was running the room, and Pete Binswanger, the writer of the episode, to send it to Joey to be proofed and published. We would get written notes the following day. But they should start writing immediately. The episode would begin prep on Friday, so we would have four days to get a script out. The staff would do another "barn raise" and then Pete and Jamie would do a pass compiling the various acts into one cohesive script that, hopefully, we could read on the flight home Thursday morning. In this new norm living in the shadow world, that was plenty of time. It was now 9pm and time for us to get dinner and some rest. Tomorrow would be jam packed with meetings from morning to night. We reconnected with Shireen and took a van back to the hotel.

During these first few months, it felt like every day brought unexpected news which was very often a problem that needed to be solved asap. This morning we were informed by Greg that the budget for the episode currently being filmed was $500,000 over budget. Matt Hastings had no idea. We were all shocked. How did this happen? There was nothing we could do since the show was already almost completed, but moving forward this would create a hole we would need to dig ourselves out of. It is common for premieres and finales to go over budget, sometimes intentionally, with planned cost savings on subsequent shows making up for the overage. But episode 202, which was starting production in two days, wasn't exactly a low budget affair. There would need to be trims. The sequence where Jace goes on a mission with Valentine to kidnap a werewolf would have to be scrubbed. The werewolf would simply appear on the ship afterwards. Greg said that was a good idea, and we told Shireen to omit the scenes in the next draft that we would publish tonight after the tech scout. The tech scout is usually done two days before an episode shoots, and involves most of the department heads and key crew members piling into a bus with the director and driving out to the locations that will be used for the show. The director then explains his plan for shooting so there are no major surprises on the day. The tech scout continues onto the sets until every scene in the script has been completed. Shireen would head out for the day with Andy Wolk and the crew and we would begin our meetings.

Michael Reisz popped in first. Any trepidation we had about it being weird between us vanished immediately. Michael too grew up in Los Angeles, a few years younger than us, and we knew many of the same people. As us Jews like to say, Michael is a total mensch. A sweet man full of positivity who had nothing bad to say about anyone. He was clearly exhausted from the last month of prepping and shooting this show and the drama that transpired during it all. To make matters worse, his air-conditioning broke down in his hotel room during the shoot, but thanks to his shrewd lobbying (Michael used to be a lawyer) he got an upgrade to the presidential suite that Will Smith was living in during the making of SUICIDE SQUAD. We told Michael that we understood if he wanted to step away from the show. We wouldn't take it personally. He had worked with Ed Decter on several shows before and would understandably be upset. But we wanted him to stay and continue to run the writer's room. He knew the staff intimately and they were all fans of his. The last thing we wanted to do was blow up the chemistry they had built. Michael was nothing but gracious. He loved the show and wanted to do whatever he could to support it. If we wanted him to stay, he would. We were thrilled and thanked him for all the great work he did on 201.

Kat was first on the call sheet and the first of our meetings. She bounced into the office in work-out clothes and a ponytail, full of her sweet, midwestern charm. She wasn't shooting that day but like many of the other actors, she liked to train on her days off. The show required a lot of physical exertion during the array of action scenes, and all the actors were dedicated to say the least. They weren't just working out; they were learning martial arts skills that they used to do some of their own stunts. Kat was only nineteen, but you'd never know it. Mature beyond her years, she began performing on Broadway at the age of fourteen and managed to graduate from college when she was an ancient seventeen. She was mature beyond her years and our years combined. Kat had read all of the books in the Mortal Instrument series and knew them from front to back. She was a true fan of the material, and was fiercely protective of her character, Clary Fairchild, reminding us that millions of fans around the world were protective as well (as we would quickly learn thanks to the Twittersphere). We were impressed and told her how eager we were to hear her opinions and thoughts about Clary. Many showrunners don't like to empower actors for fear of them running amok and doing their own thing instead of listening to direction. But we've found that we get much better performances from actors who feel deeply invested in the scenes and the show as a whole. We encouraged Kat to call us or send us emails if ideas popped into her head. Our policy with all the actors was that if they had thoughts or ideas about a line or a scene in general, they could email us whenever they'd like up to a few hours after the table read. Then the script was locked. We didn't encourage changing lines during the shoot (although there will always be exceptions), but once they knew their input would be respected, they felt deeply empowered and driven to deliver their best performance possible.

We explained to Kat and the rest of the cast that we wanted to deepen the emotion of the show. We were going to do more scenes with fewer characters where the scenes would be more about the characters and less about the plot. We wanted them to wake up excited about going to work - about creating magic and allowing the audience to feel the same emotions these characters are feeling. Kat's face lit up as we spoke about our love and appreciation for actors. We always consider the cast to be our partners, which is music to any thespian's ears. I'm in continual awe of actors and their ability to emote genuine truth on cue. There is nothing like watching an actor perform on set, under the bright lights, a camera lens a mere feet from their face as they do their work. After Broadway, Kat had cut her teeth on a number of Disney Channel shows and her craft was tight and disciplined. I could see there was much farther she and the character would grow. Without telling her exactly what was going to transpire, we told Kat that Clary was going to undergo an unimaginable tragedy that would forever thrust her into adulthood and force her character to become more mature. As she smiled with intrigue, a knock on the door interrupted. The next actor was here.

Dominic Sherwood, clad in a baseball cap and T-shirt, wasn't working that day either, so his British accent was free to fly in full force. Sincere and articulate, Dom was a serious actor who went as far as writing a journal in character as Jace. He hadn't read the books because he wanted to experience the stories firsthand just like his character was doing on the show. He took his action work extremely seriously and prided himself on doing as many stunts as possible. He also viewed the parabatai bond his character shared with Alec with great reverence. He felt like it was such a unique relationship and should be explored as much as we could. As close friends who also shared a special bond, Darren and I completely agreed and excitedly told them that in the upcoming episodes 202 and 203 the parabatai bond would play a huge role. He was pumped. We also told him we wanted to lean into the cocky, sarcastic side of Jace once he returned from his sojourn with Valentine and things returned to normal, or as normal as life can be in the shadow world. We thought Dom showed great comic timing in season one and wanted to exploit it whenever we could.

Alberto Rosende bounded in next, right off the set and still in Simon's T-shirt, jacket and jeans. Alberto was brimming with his infectious, positive energy that he carried wherever he goes. His work in season one really impressed us - his ability to go from humor to deep pathos showed great range. He had graduated from NYU right before booking the show, but his craft showed a maturity well beyond that. Growing up in Florida the son of Cuban parents, Alberto's passion vibrated with each word he spoke. He was a musician in real life, and we excitedly told him that we wanted music to play a bigger role in Simon's life in season two. When Simon played "Forever Young" in the coffee shop on season one, I admittedly rolled my eyes. Because Simon was a graphic novel writer with a creative mind, we thought we should make him a songwriter who could write songs that would help underscore the character's emotion. Like Kat, Alberto too had read all the books and knew them well. He was full of questions about the adaptation but at that point all we knew was Simon was going to become a daylighter at the end of season 2a (the first ten episodes) which would then introduce an entirely new set of issues. Alberto left with a wide smile.

Next up was Harry Shum, dressed head to toe in his Magnus wardrobe, eyeliner included. I was a huge fan of Harry's from Glee and was starstruck as soon as he walked through the door. My daughter and I bonded over that show, and the character that Harry played, the perennial underdog Mike Chang, was one of our favorite characters. So of course, I took out my phone and asked for a quick selfie with me to send to my daughter. He warmly obliged. We spoke about Glee, and the huge wave he rode so successfully for so many years. I was also a fan of dance and in awe of Harry's talent as a dancer. We wanted to use those skills with Magnus, as it was totally conceivable if not probable that Magnus Bane was a killer dancer through the centuries. Speaking of Magnus, we told Harry how much we loved his humorous side, but we yearned to go deeper with him. The fact that he's lived for so long and experienced so much tragedy felt underexplored in season one, and because we're both full of adolescent angst that never really went away, we wanted to lean into that much more in season two. The notion of Magnus finding the blade in 202 that his mother used to kill himself was a new idea that we loved setting up and paying off later. As funny as Magnus was, he was also the character that was the most layered due to his long and storied history. We couldn't wait to write his journey, and Harry could clearly feel our enthusiasm. We also felt that his relationship with Alec could be explored on a deeper level. Season one was their introduction and it was full of moving moments that were my favorite scenes of that season. But the kiss at Alec's wedding in season one, as much as I loved the moment, felt like it came out of nowhere and suddenly advanced the relationship to a place that we didn't feel was earned. We wanted to see the awkwardness of a first date and the strange courtship that would follow from both of their perspectives. It was a relationship we were excited to write. Harry felt our excitement and we felt his. It was going to be an awesome collaboration.

Emeraude Toubia strode through the door in her Isabelle Lightwood look -- high heels, all black, fire red lipstick. She had just shot a scene and was still amped from the adrenaline flow of acting. She seemed excited to meet us. We could tell she was an actor who operated on a visceral, emotional level and didn't overthink things. When we told her we wanted Izzy to kick more ass and had a scene coming up in 202 where she does just that, her face lit up. We also told her that because Izzy always portrays herself as strong and in control, we wanted to explore the issue of addiction when she uses Yin Fen to treat an injury. We thought this would be an interesting layer to the character and make her even stronger when she came out of it on the other side. As an actor she would be challenged because she would be doing something so different from any work she had done before. But Em was game, like she always was. We also talked about the flashbacks that we were doing with a little Izzy, showing how strong she was even back then growing up with two soldier brothers. Emeraude was so excited and vowed to do whatever we wanted her to do. She trusted us completely, and her confidence was comforting, especially when we were essentially flying by the seat of our pants.

The alpha of the New York wolfpack came next. In sweats and a t-shirt, Isaiah Mustafa wasn't shooting that day and appeared totally relaxed. Isaiah was a seasoned pro who had been in the business awhile and knew how blessed he was to be occupying the shoes of Luke Garroway. We had only known him from his work in the Old Spice commercials and thought he had killer comic timing and a smile that lit up the galaxy. We wanted to give Luke more of a sense of humor to mine those skills and deepen his character. Using sarcasm and humor to hide the pain and tragedy of living in the shadow world always appealed to us. We told him about his upcoming banana pancakes joke in the next episode in a scene with his police partner Alaric. We also mentioned that Luke was about to lose someone very dear to him and we wanted to explore how a werewolf deals with the overwhelming emotion of grief. We talked about exploring Luke's family and his connection to the Iron Sisters through his sister. In general, we wanted to use him more, which is something actors always like to hear.

Matt Daddarrio was the last of our cast meetings. He had been busy shooting all day and had one last scene to do. Matt's striking, movie star looks and his late entry into acting reminded me of Tom Welling, the lead of Smallville. Matt had grown up in Manhattan, worked in finance, and had travelled the world before ever considering a career in acting. He was extremely intelligent with a vast knowledge that spread from gemology to global politics. Quirky in his own unique style, and probably a tad nervous, he wasn't one for eye contact in that initial meeting. We told him how relatable Alec was for an audience torn between obeying the social mores that they grew up with and the desire to carve out their own path. Alec's ambition inside the Clave's political strata would be directly threatened by his newfound appreciation of the Downworld through his relationship with Magnus. It was dramatic chocolate cake that I was eager to devour. Like we told Dom, we wanted to explore the parabatai bond more, which he was happy about. As we discussed with Harry, we went over our ideas about Alec's relationship with Magnus. He liked that we were slowing things down between them and excited about their first date, but it was the first time I sensed a certain amount of skepticism. I understood completely. They had all worked hard in season one to create this juggernaut with a huge, worldwide fan base, and it was understandable for one of them to wonder if we were going to screw it up in a big way. We told Matt we were here for him if he had any thoughts or ideas moving forward, and parted ways until the table read the next day.

A woman wearing a vintage Neil Diamond t-shirt peered in wanting to introduce herself. This was Margo Klewans, from Constantin Film, exuding warmth. This was the first television show she had worked on, a show she had spearheaded from the very beginning. We spoke about Neil Diamond of course. We thought the shirt might've just been a fashion statement, but no, Margo was in fact a diehard Neil Diamond fan. She could not have been nicer, and told us if there was anything we needed, she was here for us. When she was back in Los Angeles she wanted to take us out to lunch to talk in greater detail. We thanked her for her support, instantly recognizing an ally.

The tech scout returned to the studio and Shireen and Andy Wolk filled us in on the details. Andy was happy we were cutting the abduction of Gretel the wolf. It would make the tight shooting schedule more doable. We discussed the casting choices for the supporting roles. We always asked the writer and director for their choices before we weighed in and it seemed that we were all in agreement. Shireen was going to add changes from the tech scout into the script and send us the draft in a few hours so we could tweak and publish for the table read the next day. We were interrupted by our pinging emails with the network notes for the 203 beat sheet, notes which incorporated the thoughts from Constantin and Wonderland. I am always nervous when I get notes on an outline for a script, especially when the script is already in the process of being written. But these notes brought a smile to my face. They loved the episode and recognized how emotionally powerful it was. Their thoughts were minimal and would be easy to execute in the script. Our email also pinged with the casting links for the Maia Roberts audition. We would watch and review the 202 script back at the hotel after dinner.

Casting is one of my favorite parts of the process. Writing a character on the page and then finding the perfect actor to inhabit the role can be extremely satisfying or terribly disappointing. One has to choose very carefully. We had had our share of successes and failures casting roles on the various shows we've worked on and knew that the role of Maia was hugely important. Allison Silverberg and Jonathan Clay Harris were holding auditions in Los Angeles. They had cast the series regulars for season one and crushed it in a big way. Lisa Parasyn was holding auditions in Toronto. Back in the day if we were casting a big role like this, we would be in the casting session for the finalists and meet the actors in person. This was nice because you could give them notes and they could tweak their performance in the room to better help you imagine them in the role. It was also awkward as hell if you didn't respond to the audition. There was nowhere to hide. You'd simply smile and nod and say thank you, which I hated. I tend to wear my heart on my sleeve. It's hard to hide my visceral reaction (just ask the countless annoyed writers who've worked with me over the years). Today, most casting is done over video links, which is awesome for a self-conscious guy like me.

We pulled the links from our email and saw a message from Pete with his choices but decided to wait and read them in order for us to watch Maia with fresh eyes. There were a lot of strong actors, but Alisha Wainwright was the clear stand out. She didn't look or feel like an actor. She felt real -- with a deep strength combined with a soft, honest vulnerability. She felt like Maia. But she hadn't been in much else. Her IMDB page was much shorter than many of the other actors who had auditioned. There was another actress who was also good, but once we opened Pete's email and saw that Alisha was his top choice as well, it was sealed. We sent off an email to Jonathan and Allison instructing them to let the network know and hoped that the powers that be would agree on our choice.

The following day was another jam-packed extravaganza. There was the production meeting for 202, attended by the same crew who were in the concept meeting seven days ago, only now the plans were being finalized for the shoot that would begin tomorrow. It was also a chance for us to meet all the department heads in person. This meeting was followed by the tone meeting. A tone meeting is a usually lengthy discussion between the director, writer and showrunner about each scene in the script. For us it's the most important meeting in prep because it's our opportunity to communicate to the director exactly what we expect to be captured in every scene. We can fill them in on character dynamics that they might not be aware of. Luckily Andy had already done two episodes in season one so he was well versed on the characters and mythology.

Often in tone meetings we can point to a prior episode as an example of what we like but in this case there was no prior of episode that we'd done. 201 was still shooting and one couldn't really get a sense of tone watching dailies. Over troughs of dim sum, we went through every scene in detail. David Herrington, the D.P., was there as well to hear our thoughts. We knew many of the scenes had the potential to be overly earnest if executed in a certain way, and Andy had great suggestions. We tweaked a few things here and there that Shireen would incorporate into the next draft. As the tone meeting entered its third hour, we were interrupted by Greg Copeland with the news that the budgets from the various department heads had come in for episode 202 and we were still $350,000 over. I was stunned. I thought by cutting out the kidnapping scene we had solved the problem, but I was wrong. We didn't have time to focus on the cuts because the table read was starting in five minutes and that had to start on time. It was held at the lunch hour of the shooting day so there was a tight sixty-minute window to gather all the actors and read the script. We instructed Greg and Chris to slash as much as they could from the budget that wouldn't change the story and we would reconvene after the table read.

We were ushered down another brightly lit corridor into the conference room, which was now filled with every actor on the show. Normally only the series regulars are at a table read, but today the entire supporting cast was there because they all played such important roles in season one. Vanessa Matsui, who plays Dot, was there. She would play a crucial role in this episode. Nicola Emeraude, who plays Maryse, was shooting that day alongside Maxim Roy, who plays Jocelyn. Knowing how Jocelyn's fate would eventually play out, it was uncomfortably awkward. I hate keeping secrets. It's bad for everyone, but now was not the time or the place to talk about the future. We were in the moment. The telephone line was hooked up to Los Angeles, where all the executives were listening in as well as the writing staff. We see the table read as the last opportunity to make adjustments to the script, and we always sit down with the writing staff after the table read to hear thoughts and pitches for better or funnier lines. Some of the most memorable lines from the show have come from these after table-read sessions in the writer's room. Matt Hastings, fresh from directing for six hours and now on his lunch break, hurried in. The room was jam packed and we were ready to go. I read the scene description, which I knew would lend an energy and enthusiasm to the proceedings and keep the mood as light as possible. There was a sense of tension in the room that one couldn't ignore. This was the first time every one would hear how a Slavkin-Swimmer episode of Shadowhunters sounded.

And it sounded decent. People laughed when they were supposed to laugh. Simon and Magnus in India were hysterical. Lumps in throats were visible when Izzy was pleading with Alec not to risk losing consciousness to go after Jace. The cast was on the edge of their seat at the end, wondering what was going to happen next. Matt Daddario jokingly asked if he was going to die. It felt like a success but there was a pit in our stomach knowing we couldn't produce the existing script. We hurried back to our office with Shireen and Michael Reisz and hopped on the phone with the writer's room to discuss all of our ideas. They were all enthusiastic and we made a few tweaks here and there. The network sent over their notes as well, many in line with ours. We huddled with Shireen and decided what notes we wanted to use, and then she went off to implement them. She would send the file back to us for our final pass on the script, which we would do when we got back to the hotel.

We were outside headed to the make-up trailer to touch base with Kat about a note in the script when Greg and Chris gingerly approached. They'd been crunching the numbers and discovered that we can get down to budget if we dropped the India sequence, which was scheduled to shoot at an expensive location. We immediately dug in. Wasn't there some other way? Could we greatly reduce the number of extras? Or compromise on the fight club stuff and do that cheaper? Simon and Magnus going to India had to be part of the show. Hell, I'd watch a whole episode of the two of them snooping around Camille's villa. Chris

Hatcher nodded his head, as if he had something going on in the back of his head. I might have been imagining it at the time, hoping for a stroke of genius. We told them we had to go back to the hotel and write. It was getting late and we had to start on our pass through what would be the locked shooting script. We would call them in an hour to get the lowest number possible we could be over without sacrificing India. We would then reach out to the network and explain the pickle and see if they would give us extra money to cover the overage given the unique situation.

Back at the hotel, the computer flipped on and the mini bar swung open. After eating Dim Sum all day, I was starving and stressed. White cheddar cheese popcorn, dark chocolate and white wine kept me going as we entered the shadow world and began to write. Meanwhile we were waiting to hear back from the network to see what number they would agree to cover. When I say cover, I should say money they are agreeing to loan us that we will pay back to them by producing cheaper episodes down the road. But now we needed the big bucks. The latest email from Greg said we could produce the script for $200,000 over budget. Our friend Jenn Gerstenblatt was talking to Karey Burke, the Head of Original Programming at the network, to get her approval. As we waited, we wrote, tweaking lines here and there, making each other laugh. Finally at 2am East Coast time the call came in from Jenn. We could spend the extra $200,000 if we made up for it later. We promised we would and thanked her profusely. Jenn was the one who brought us into the world and her support meant a lot.

We finished the draft and hit send at 2:30 in the morning. Darren went to his room. The alarm would ring two and a half hours later for my pick-up to the airport. Our flight to L.A. left at 8am. But I couldn't sleep. I was still wired with adrenaline from the day, my brain a pachinko machine of racing thoughts. Insomnia is something I've always wrestled with, and this new job wasn't doing me any favors. Finally I fell asleep, dreaming of runes.

# THE RHYTHM OF THE HEAT

I don't often cry when reading a script, as in never, but sitting on the airplane the following morning waiting to take off, it happened. I was reading the last scene in the script for 203 aka "Parabatai Lost" when Jace recites his parabatai oath to a dying Alec, elegantly intercut with their characters as children reciting the same oath, and it brought genuine tears to my eyes - enough tears that I had to wipe my wet cheek. Granted I was suffering from severe sleep deprivation, but the moment on the page stirred me in a profound way. I knew gold when I read it, and that was gold. The whole script was strong and the entire staff contributed, but Pete had clearly done his own pass where he stream-lined the voices to make them his own. Pete is a great writer who combines humor and pathos really well - an expert at writing Simon, especially. I was pumped about the episode. Darren and I would do a pass when we got home but this script would definitely be ready to be prepped on Friday.

Something happened on that flight that's never happened to me before. Actually, two things. First off, I don't cry when I read things then receive strange glances from fellow passengers who think they're witnessing some profound emotional train wreck. Secondly, and most shockingly, as soon as we were airborne, I laid back in my fancy first class seat that turned into a flat-bed and fell asleep within seconds. When I woke up, the pilot was announcing that we were about to land in Los Angeles. I slept through an entire flight.

After a quick shower at home I was back in the office for lunch in the writer's room to fill them in on our experience in Toronto and begin the early discussions for 204. Pete was flying up to Toronto that day to spearhead prep for 203, Shireen was in Toronto on set for 202, and Michael would be coming down the following day after 201 wrapped, so the room was smaller than normal, which was unusual for us. We came up on a show where writers didn't go to set. Smallville was shot in Vancouver, and writers would go to set only on special occasions - like an actor making their directing debut. We were fortunate to write and be on set for both Tom Welling and Michael Rosenbaum's directing debuts. But on that show writers worked in a writer's room writing and creating, and if the director was prepped properly, there would be little need for a writer on set. As a director myself, I appreciated that concept. I didn't like a writer looking over my shoulder when I was directing, giving me notes on my notes. As a writer, I always felt uncomfortable on set -- like an intruder into a creative process that I wasn't a part of. I feel so awkward giving a director notes because I know how it feels on the other side. But the network wanted a writer on set, and all the writers loved getting away and travelling to Toronto for two weeks to be part of the production. We weren't about to change up the mojo. It was a large writing staff anyway. There were plenty of brilliant minds in that room cooking up magic.

We knew Jace in the City of Bones would be featured in 204 and that would be a great opportunity to do some cool world building. The Silent Brothers in season one felt a bit goofy to us, but in the right setting -- like a prison for disgraced Shadowhunters, with their faces cast in shadow, lit by only fire-light -- they could be horrifying. We liked the idea of Jace coming across Hodge from season one and having to face the soul sword tribunal, coming head to head with his inner thoughts, especially those regarding Clary. We also knew this would be the episode where Jocelyn died, and our procedural "day in the life" of a shadowhunter story could fold into that. Alec and Clary would investigate a virus that infects people and causes them to murder. That virus would get into the institute and infect Alec, who would then tragically kill Jocelyn under the influence. The stories would "kiss" nicely and the ramifications would be devastating for everyone involved. At first we thought it would be awesome if Clary was the one who became infected and, in a shocking turn, killed her own mom, but the network rightfully thought it was a step too far and suggested our back up, Alec, would be just as powerful. We understood completely. In a nod to the books, Taylor Mallory suggested Valentine be the one who created the virus in order to distract the shadowhunters from the breakout at the City of Bones. Ideas were flowing like the River Jordan. Jamie Gorenberg was writing the episode and her mind was racing a million miles a minute.

All was good, except for the pit in our stomachs about killing off Jocelyn. We knew that many fans of the books and the show were going to hate the idea. We knew we would get endless amounts of hateful tweets sent in our direction. But we also knew we had to make the show we wanted to make, rather than cater our creative decisions to the fandom. If we did that, we would simply be following the books word for word, chapter after chapter, which would be boring for everyone, creative personnel and audience alike. We had to make the show for ourselves and trust that our taste corresponded with the taste of the fandom.

We went upstairs, blocked out the sun, and cranked Bon Iver. Since we began writing together thirty years ago, we usually wrote with music playing, music that we knew and weren't distracted by. Bon Iver seemed to go with our mood and the show, and it became the recurring soundtrack for our first months in the shadow world. We quickly finished and sent the script off to Pete and Joey to review. This would be the draft going to the network, the second episode they would read from the new regime.

The concept meeting for 203 Skyped-in crystal clear over our computer monitor, glare no longer an issue thanks to the curtains. I immediately recognized Greg Smith, the director of the episode and a former actor who was one of the stars of EVERWOOD, a show that aired on the WB at the same time as Smallville.

Pete Binswanger sat next to Greg, comfortable as ever in the world of production. The cast and crew loved Pete from season one, and based on his writing and charming confidence, I recognized a future director in the making. Matt Hastings was there, refreshed and now occupying the role of a producer, which was vital during the prep of the show. Matt and his team reinvented the look of the show and the way it was shot, and his involvement in prep would help shape the director's vision in order to fit the new design.

Because he was directing the massive premiere, Matt couldn't be as involved in the prep of 202, but on 203 he was there every step of the way. The script was written to be done at a lower budget. The only issue was the visual effects of the wolves. Wolf shots were the most expensive item on the VFX menu because of the detail and time involved in creating them, particularly their fur coat, made of countless individual hairs. It was a painstaking process to try to make them as natural-looking as possible. And as we quickly learned, fur ain't easy, and neither is the physics -- when the wolves moved, they tended to look like they were floating instead of putting their weight down. Our visual effects team told us they could get it done right for a price, and it would look amazing. The notes from the network came later that day on the 203 script and they loved it. They liked the new direction of the show and all was good in the world. And most importantly, they loved Alisha Wainwright's audition and were thrilled with our choice. We had our Maia.

Our email inboxes were now a continuous flood of incoming photos and drawings that needed to be approved. Wardrobe photos of the cast members modelling the choices for each episode was a constant, as were pictures of locations and concept drawings for new sets. There were also make-up tests, hair tests, prop choices, casting links and preliminary stunt videos. Matt weighed in as well, but we had final approval, which required us to stop what we were doing and focus on the countless decisions we were making every hour on the hour. For wardrobe, we knew from our experience on GUILT that the network had strong opinions and wanted to be involved in those decisions. We were happy to defer to them on all things clothing related. They had great taste.

Prior to us coming aboard, Matt Hastings informed us that he had made a deal with the network to bring on his old friend Sam Hollander to write original music for the show that could be released later to the public. We had never heard of an agreement like that on a TV show unless it was a show specifically about music, like SMASH, which Sam had written the music for. But because we wanted to turn Simon into an original songwriter and showcase his music on the show, we were thrilled. Sam is an enormously gifted songwriter and producer who's worked with everyone from Panic at the Disco to Carole King and has had enormous success along the way. We sat down to meet Sam in our cramped office with Matt sitting in over Skype and pitched our vision for Simon the songwriter as a cross between Ed Sheeran and Bon Iver. Sam totally got it and went on to write a number of songs for Simon and for the show in general.

That weekend Jamie was off to begin the outline for 204. She had been a playwright and wrote for many sit-coms and dramedies. It didn't take long to realize how bright she was, and how deep her mind worked. I could tell she was anxious about writing in this new genre and I told her to relax and have fun. Writing genre was no different than writing any other human drama. It's all about the emotion. Don't think so much. Let it flow. We had wine and cheese with all the writers and support staff that late Friday afternoon, a tradition we picked up from Liz Tigelar, who was running LIFE UNEXPECTED in the same studio we were shooting Melrose Place. Jamie only had a few sips as she had her long nightly commute ahead of her. Sure enough, come Monday she delivered a strong outline and a strong draft. Alec's "Impossible just means try again" is a classic Jamie G line. She totally got the romance and sturm and drang of the shadow world.

Alisha Wainwright came in for a meeting before heading out to Toronto to shoot 203. Relaxed, wearing glasses and a sundress, she was the most un-actory actor I'd ever met. There were no airs about her whatsoever, no "on" persona like so many actors had. She was totally natural and at ease with herself, charming and smart at the same time. She was so excited about playing Maia - a strong woman, a victim of abuse, who had overcome enormous obstacles to set her own path in a dangerous world. She hadn't been auditioning for too long, but she knew this was a great role, and expressed her gratitude by bringing us candy from her recent trip to Hawaii. We didn't know exactly how many episodes she'd be in, but based on the role she played in the books, we knew it would be a lot. When she spoke about her background studying botany in college in Florida and even working as a botanist for a short time after graduating, we came up with the idea of Maia wanting to be a marine biologist. We liked the idea that Maia Roberts would have this career goal before she got turned into a werewolf, a goal that she would continue to chase while juggling life in the shadow world. She was eager to hear as much as she could about her character, and we wanted her to meet the writing staff. So we led her down the rickety stairwell into the room and introduced her to everyone. She was charming as could be, offering more candy for the writers. She was raised well.

203 began production and the dailies looked fantastic. Greg Smith's shotmaking was strong and the performances were all awesome. As we expected, Alisha was incredible. Whenever she spoke you simply believed her. But we couldn't appreciate how complete the visual makeover really was until we finally were able to watch the director's cut for 201. Matt Hastings took extra time to get his cut exactly right before anyone saw it and for good reason. He wanted it to be jaw-droppingly great, and it was. The cut fulfilled our expectations and more. Even though there were no visual effects yet, the film looked beautiful. It was darker and moodier and cooler. The acting felt more adult. The weapons looked badass. The action sequences took my breath away. Jace falling under Valentine's control felt real. Clary and Izzy training together left me delightfully dizzy. The ship was staggering in scope. Clary and Simon reminiscing about their friendship in the boat basin was heartwarming. We immediately called Matt and gushed. He had taken the show to another level and we couldn't have been happier. Our only note was that the action sequence in the beginning of the show went on forever. Because it was a minute and a half over, I thought it was a no brainer to take the time out of that sequence. It didn't affect the story and there was so much greatness already built into the action that the audience wouldn't miss the cuts.

Like us, the network loved 201. It was a show everyone was proud of, as they were of the shooting script for 204, now titled "Day of Wrath" from a chapter in one of the books. But they had more notes on this script. The writing staff had witnessed the previous regime battle the network and that relationship had turned acrimonious. Our relationship with the network was much more harmonious, partly because they just hired us and were rooting for us to succeed, but also because we felt that their thoughts were almost always spot on. When we did disagree, they would usually back off and trust our instincts. Many writers and showrunners look down on studio and network executives who give them notes, sometimes disregarding their thoughts before they even hear them. But Darren and I love to hear other people's ideas about our material, especially smart, experienced professionals, and most creative executives in television are very smart. They want to make a great show just like we do. And we all agreed the shooting script for 204 was in good shape.

Margo Klewans, now back in Los Angeles after being on set in Toronto for 201, was kind enough to invite Darren and I to lunch to celebrate the positive changes and talk about the show. She chose the Chateau Marmont, a fancy hotel in West Hollywood most widely known as the site of John Belushi's tragic death. We've had a few lunch meetings over the years there, and it's not uncommon to see a movie star. Last time it was Charlize Theron. This time I was keeping my eyes wide open. We were seated on the beautiful garden patio and immediately noticed another kind of star. There sat Karey Burke, the Head of Original Programming at Freeform, having lunch with Tom Ascheim, the President of the network. They waved us over and could not have been more glowing about the show. They had seen the cut of 201 and were in awe of the new look. Karey had just read 204 and loved the most recent changes to the script. They told us to keep doing what we were doing and sent us back to finish our lunch, but not without sending over three glasses of champagne. I immediately recognized that this was a storybook moment in my own tiny slice of Hollywood lore. The head of a network buying you a glass of champagne to toast your success was one of those things that didn't happen often, especially to guys like us.

When we returned to our office, in a rare moment that shattered our vow only to look at what was immediately ahead of us, we actually allowed ourselves to think about the future for a second. Unless we screwed things up in a major way, which was of course always possible, we realized Shadowhunters would probably get another season. And some writers would want to move on to something else. It was only natural. Michael Reisz intimated that this would be his last season in our first meeting together. There was one writer we had worked with before who we knew would be absolutely exceptional in the shadow world. They had never been the number two on a show before, but I knew they were ready for it.

Bryan Q. Miller was a young intern on Smallville when we first met him. A clerk at a bookstore by day and a graduate film student by night, Q was a comic book aficionado and a genre junkie. He was also a talented graphic artist who designed our show and tell presentation for our Smallville season 8 pitch to Peter Roth at Warner Brothers. He quickly rose from intern to to writer's assistant to staff writer. I was lucky enough to supervise his first hour of television, which he absolutely crushed. He was a talent to be reckoned with. Years later we brought him onto Defiance, then Dominion, then Guilt. He wasn't just a genre writer. He was a great writer with a lightning quick mind that was an ever-flowing fountain of ideas. Q was finishing up a season on SLEEPY HOLLOW in December. Realizing a Shadowhunters season three was probable, we wondered if we could bring Q in as a consulting producer in January, working part time for the remainder of season 2B. At that point the room would probably be breaking episode 214, but he would still be invaluable, and the hire would enable us to secure his services in season three as a co-executive producer. It seemed like a good idea and the network agreed, so I called Q and broached the idea. He was intrigued and we told him we would keep him posted as we got closer to the end of the year.

The story for episode 205 came together as organically as almost any episode I had ever worked on in television. It was the first episode of season two where we didn't feel like we were in a frantic rush, fighting the clock to get a script out in time. We knew this episode had the potential to be deeply moving. The death of Jocelyn hung like a pall over all the characters, and this would be an awesome opportunity to explore how each of them deals with grief. Clary going to a warlock to try to bring her mom back was one of the first threads thrown about. One of the first images I had in my mind was the dead raven being brought back to life and then later coming back to feverishly peck at the window until it shattered so it could swoop in and attack. I've always been horrified by birds flying in a house. It's happened to me before and I am still chilled to the bone to this day. The idea of death and birth being connected under the roof of this strange woman was intriguing. Iris Rouse kidnapping women and impregnating them with a demon to increase the warlock population was exciting but also very sick and depraved - in the best possible way. We knew some people would have an issue with the dark, twisted turn the story took, but we liked it and didn't want to censor ourselves. We wanted to embrace it. I also liked the idea of Clary being in such a horrible, desperate situation when she created her first rune. Clary being able to create her own runes was always a part of the books that fascinated me, and I looked forward to doing it in the show. The sunlight rune would be something that Jace would witness and then they would share this secret.

Clary's awkward pairing with Alec in this episode felt like a great way to untangle the tension between them from the last episode. It was also a way to explore the force of Alec's guilt and how it made him make questionable decisions. On the way to work one morning I imagined Alec standing on the Institute rooftop shooting glamoured arrows into the stratosphere, over and over until his hands bled, as a way of dealing with his guilt. When I parked my car I saw Geoff Leavitt the VFX guru stepping out of his car. I excitedly told him my idea and asked if we could do something like that within the budget of the show. He assured me we could, and I headed into my office feeling the rush of coming up with a cool idea.

The idea of Simon lighting a candle and reciting the Mourner's Kaddish in honor of Jocelyn gave me goosebumps. Although I'm not religious, I was born Jewish and feel that the Judaic culture is very much a part of me. The chance to explore Jewish customs and traditions through Simon Lewis was thrilling and an opportunity to expose the culture to millions of fans around the world. In the beginning, Simon was the character I related to the most, and 205 was the first time we could delve into his family life and see his attempts to balance the shadow world with his home world. The idea of "coming out of the coffin" and telling his mom that he was a vampire felt like a particularly relevant analogy for LGBQT fans of the show and would be emotional for everyone watching the episode. That scene remains one of my favorites of the series.

Iris Rouse was a wonderfully effective villain because she believed she was doing the right thing. Her midwestern charm and zany humor came directly from Zac Hug and his Ohio upbringing. Before we arrived, a writing order was established by the previous showrunner where each writer was assigned their episode in advance, and 205 was assigned to Zac. Fortunately for us, it was the ideal episode for him to write. Zac not only had an offbeat, quirky sense of humor but he also was extremely empathetic with a beautiful beating heart who could deftly handle Clary's grief. Zac came up with the title "Dust and Shadows" from the book, and even named Madzie after his lucky niece.

We loved the idea of Iris being the mother figure to a little child warlock with gills, and we knew how touching it would be for Alec to come across the little girl and try to make conversation. The tender side of Alec was my favorite part of his character - the side that would never judge someone because they're different but rather celebrate their difference. "Cool gills" is one of my all-time favorite moments of the series. At that point we had no idea how big of a role Madzie would play in the long run. That's the beauty of writing television over several seasons. Once you see how well something works you can continue the story in interesting and different ways. In this case, the casting for both roles was perfect. Stephanie Belding brought just the right amount of sincerity and quirkiness so that it was feasible that Clary would trust her, especially in her cloud of grief. Of course, later we would see how scary she really was. Stephanie played both sides with equal honesty. Ariana Williams, who played Madzie, was barely four when we saw her audition. She wasn't exactly an actor at that age but that face - that face was to die for. She was beyond adorable. Darren had concerns over her ability level and inexperience, but I promised him she would be fantastic. I knew in my heart of hearts the audience would love her.

As with almost every script, we did a pass on 205, and that writing process was extremely emotional. Because the show dealt with grief, it released a floodgate of memories of all the moments I've lost someone that meant a lot to me. We had split up the scenes and I was lucky enough to work on the funeral sequence. It was in the evening in my home study, tears in my eyes as I had Clary falter when asked to state her mother's full name to the Silent Brothers. All she could mutter were the words "mom". My writing was interrupted by the ringing of my cell phone. It was Kat McNamara calling from Toronto. She was at the film festival at TIFF and had an idea for a line change in an upcoming script. Her timing was eerie. I immediately told her what I was doing and promised that she would have a special experience shooting this episode. To this day it is one of my favorite Clary stories in the series.

Sallie Richardson-Whitfield, an actress Matt Hastings had worked with on EUREKA who made her directorial debut on that show, was scheduled to direct this episode. All the directors had already been hired for season two when we started. Usually showrunners had input into who directed the show, but after seeing 201, we trusted Matt's taste wholeheartedly and supported all of his choices. The script was in great shape, with a story that was constantly unfolding in surprising ways. If executed well, the funeral would be so powerful. I couldn't wait to watch Isabelle try yin fen to try to heal herself for her journey to the Iron Sisters, and then gradually get addicted, all at the hands of that manipulative son of a bitch Victor Aldertree. The idea of Luke naked in the forest, grief-stricken, howling at the moon as he fights the instinct to turn, was a terrific push off to the next episode. After the tone meeting with Salli, we felt like we were now making the show we wanted to make. We were finding our rhythm and it was all beginning to click. It almost felt too easy… and then we got the call.

# THE FIRST HICCUP

Whenever a lot of people are calling together to talk to us, it's either a great sign or a terrible one. In this case, it was the entire team - the network, Constantin, Matt Hastings and Wonderland - and it wasn't great news. They had all watched the cut for 202, and while there were moments that they liked, they felt like it was a letdown after the premiere and didn't feel it had the same cinematic flare. The story moved too slow and the pacing felt flat. Ouch. We knew when we first saw the director's cut that it felt different than the premiere, but that was to be expected given the strange circumstances. Andy is a great director but he and David, the new cinematographer, didn't shoot the show with the same visual style because it wasn't invented yet. Matt was basically directing a new pilot with a new style while this episode was being prepped. But I still liked Andy's cut quite a bit. The heart and soul were all there. The story tracked. But the pacing did feel off. The editor was from season one, and the cut didn't pop with the frenetic energy of 201. It also did look different. It was brighter and less moody. The framing and camera movement were a bit more conservative. But I wasn't prepared for such a negative reaction from the powers that be. They sent over pages of notes. Matt sent over pages of notes. And Darren and I decided to bring new eyes into the editing bay.

Pete Gvodas, the editor who cut 201, had decided to move on and do the pilot for SIREN, but he had a week before he started that job, and we asked him if he would do a pass on the show and incorporate the notes. He agreed, and we tightened the show into a knot that came out to a 38-minute running time. Our target for broadcast on Freeform was 42 minutes and thirty seconds including the recap, but they were fine if a show was a little under. Netflix on the other hand required a certain length, and we were under. Darren and I asked Matt if he could shoot a few additional scenes to not only get to time but also give the episode more emotional depth and drive. He was totally game, and we were off to the races. Knowing Jocelyn's fate, we added the scene with her and Luke outside by his car on the search for Clary. We also added two scenes with Isabelle and Alec on the hunt for Jace. One on location, which added drive but admittedly wasn't one of our finest moments, and another scene in the Institute, where we hit home how affected Alec is by the possibility of losing his parabatai. We recognized early on that Matt Daddario was at his best when he was deeply emotional. Of course, he also had great comic timing and was good in other scenes, but he shined when Alec had a lump in his throat. In addition, Matt Hastings wanted to build out of some of the action moments on the boat by shooting characters on green screen and inserting them into the existing footage.

These new scenes were cut into the show by David E.K. Abramson, the quiet, unassuming visual effects editor. After working with David on the recap of season one, which required a tremendous amount of knowledge and finesse, we quickly realized how unbelievably talented he was. Not only was David lightning fast on his Avid and an outstanding editor, but he was one of the smartest people I'd ever met, and I've met a lot of smart people over the years. After Pete left, David took over the editing duties on 202, creating the amazing montage of visions that Jocelyn displayed for Clary when she explained how Valentine experimented on her during her pregnancy. David also built the awesome sequence of the visions of a destructive future that Clary showed to Jace. He was brilliant. After his outstanding work on 202 helping us deliver a show that the powers that be thought was suitable for broadcast, we hired him as a full-time editor and brought him into the rotation. 205 would be the first episode he would edit on his own, and he gave it his all. In his editor's cut, when Alec was shooting arrows, David designed a billboard that the arrow hit in a way that made the letters spell "Demon". God knows how long it took him to make that happen. It was meticulously executed, but it wasn't the tone we were trying to set. We never wanted to wink at the material, like Buffy did so beautifully. Like the books, we wanted to try and keep it grounded at all times. David learned the tone quickly and went on to crush that episode and many, many more.

At the end of the day there were three editors on 202 and the post-production period was longer than any episode besides a pilot we've ever worked on. But it was all worth it in the end. Once the visual effects were in and the music was locked, I was all in. The set-up of baby Jonathan in the garden where his eyes go black and the leaves wither was an awesome way to kick off the show. All the actors gave great performances. It might not be my favorite of the series, but I'm proud of the end result. It was a crisis averted. But at that time there was always another right around the corner.

On my thirty-minute commute in the morning, my hope was always to chill and listen to music, but because of production happening three hours later, phone calls sometimes interrupted the reverie, and those calls were usually not the calmest, relaxing sort. On this particular morning it was Jayne Bieber, the head of physical production for the network, and Gary Mrowca, the head of post-production, calling to inform us that the visual budget for the show was off the hook over budget, to the tune of four hundred thousand dollars. From our first day Jayne and Gary had been extremely supportive, and they were as nice as can be as they told us it had to come down. They understood that the wolves were the most expensive item on the menu and were necessary for 203, but the overage needed to be made up. So we made a pact moving forward to approach the stories in the room knowing we had to greatly reduce that number until we made up the difference. It took a while, but the subsequent episodes don't appear like they suffered in that department. The Jocelyn funeral sequence in 202 is one of my favorite visual effect moments in the series.

Episode 206 was going to be written by Allison Rymer. We were all excited about Clary and Isabelle going to the Citadel and meeting the Iron Sisters. Any opportunity to world build and design something that's never been seen before is always thrilling. John Rakich and his location team found a grand castle in Toronto with a wading pool in back. It worked perfectly for the story, when Clary and Isabelle would be tested to see if they had demonic blood. The idea of Simon and Maia pairing up to track down Luke in the forest allowed us to get into character-based scenes where they could begin to get to know each other. Their story still had drive because they had to get to Luke before he turned and killed innocent people. Those innocent people generated much discussion, as did any of the countless decisions we had to make. Even though it was a bit cheesy and a trope, I liked the young couple making out in the tent. It felt like a good old-fashioned horror story. Continuing our love of flashbacks, seeing Luke help Maia the night she first turned felt so right and would help us understand why she was so intent on helping Luke now.

The Malec date would be the third story. Most Shadowhunters episodes had an A, B and C story, not necessarily in order of importance or screen time. We've done a fourth story from time to time, but it's never a good idea in a 42-minute time frame. The pacing always suffers. On Smallville, Ken Horton, the executive producer in charge of post for the first seven seasons, taught me the importance of the space between the dialog - the exchanging of looks between characters to enhance the emotional impact. A Shadowhunters episode always benefited from emotional moments having time to breathe. In the early talks about the Malec date, there was talk about having their night become interrupted by the main plot, so Alec and/or Magnus would have to branch off to help the gang. But my instinct was to make it solely about the characters and what they discover about one another rather than attach it to any plot. It wasn't popular but I held my ground. Darren and I had a long-standing agreement that if one of us was super passionate about an idea, we should do it, and this was one of those moments. I also went up against the tide when I suggested that 17,000 was the number of men

Magnus had slept with over the centuries. There was much discussion about what number was appropriate, but at the end of the day the words 17,000 sounded kinda funny.

Matt and Harry were understandably anxious moving forward in the Malec relationship. They had no idea what was going to transpire and had many questions. They wanted to meet with us the following week when we were back in Toronto, and we gladly agreed. We would meet them for dinner with Matt Hastings right after we landed. When we touched down, I was somehow sent to the immigration office while Darren sailed right on through to meet our van. I was lucky enough to find myself in the back of an endless line of tourists who had just landed. This was going to take 45 minutes at least. I texted Darren to go ahead to the restaurant, and I would meet them when I got out. They could start the conversation without me. An hour later I raced to the waiting van and drove to the restaurant only to have the driver get lost. I was cursed. Finally I arrived at the small Italian place, rolling suitcase in tow. Matt, Harry, Darren and Hastings were at a table patiently waiting for me. I apologized profusely. Matt was unshaven in a baseball cap, unrecognizable as Alec Lightwood. Harry too was low key in a t-shirt and jeans. We ordered wine and dinner and began to talk.

They too felt their first kiss put the two characters way ahead of where the relationship was really at and liked this slower approach. Now they were worried that we were going too fast. The things that were said on the first date and the idea that they would have sex in the next episode - it felt rushed to them. We understood, but we also felt in order to keep the relationship real, grounded and honest, after what these two men had gone through, they would have sex. If we dragged it out longer, it would feel contrived and unrealistic given where they were at in their lives and the way they felt about each other. They also cautioned us to avoid making choices based solely on what we thought the fans wanted most. The Malec fandom was huge and loud and full of creative people who had their own ideas of the relationship. We assured them that we would follow our own creative instincts. Writing this relationship and digging into the conflicts between these two disparate characters was one of the things that excited us most about the job. It was one of our favorite parts of the show, and we would treat it with the respect it deserved. When they brought up the idea of contributing ideas of their own, we welcomed it with open arms. Sure enough when we got back to L.A. they sent us a rewrite of the beginning of the scene in 207 when Magnus and Alec come through the doors of Magnus' apartment carrying shopping bags after their trip to Tokyo. The fatty tuna run was all Matt and Harry.

The writer's draft of 206 aka "Iron Sisters" came in particularly strong. Allison Rymer was just a staff writer, but she'd been a script coordinator on many shows before that, and her attention to detail was outstanding. The story of Clary falling asleep with peanut butter in her hair was pure Ally. We cast a great actress, Lisa Berry, to play Cleophas, Luke's sister and the anchor of the story. Mike Rohl was a director we had worked with before on Smallville, and we were ultra-confident in his abilities to take a great script and bring it to film.

Greg Smith's director's cut for 203 arrived late at night. Since I had to drop my daughter off at school super early, I made it a habit back then to get to work early before anyone else was there so I could watch a cut or write by myself alone and undisturbed. That morning I closed the blackout curtains and watched Greg Smith's masterful work. I was blown away. It even looked better than the premiere. Edited by Nate Easterling, the pacing was excellent, and the show was full of great, cinematic moments and incredibly emotional performances. The ending could not have been more moving. Tears streamed down my face as Jace was led out of Magnus' apartment - thank God I was alone. Darren came in soon after having watched at home and felt the same way. It was a great episode of the show. We were off to the races.

# MEET THE PRESS

In early October we returned to Canada on our way to the New York Comic-Con to film a few behind the scenes interviews on the Institute set. These things were always awkward for me. I'm not an "in front of the camera" kind of guy. I'm way too self-conscious. But we managed to get through it with minimal pain. We were also there to meet Cassie Clare in person. Cassie had flown up to Toronto to see the new sets, and the cast and crew honored her with a dim sum luncheon in the Jade Wolf. Kat presented Cassie with her very own stele, made by the wonderfully talented props master Tony Smokes and mounted in a beautiful glass frame. Cassie seemed deeply moved, as did Kat. Afterwards we all went into the conference room to watch the season premiere, still in its rough stages but with a few visual effects here and there. We wanted Cassie and the cast to see their great work and have a better foundation to talk about season two with the press at Comic-Con. As they watched, we stole glances at a few awestruck faces, and when it was over everyone applauded. It was time to go to Comic-Con.

Because the actor's shooting schedules varied, they were all due to arrive in New York at different times. Darren and I flew from Toronto with Dom,

Alberto and Isaiah. Over a beer in the lounge, we got to relax and hang out, away from work. I was immediately taken with how down to earth they all seemed, and their genuine excitement about going to the con. They loved hanging out with the fans. When we arrived in New York, Dom acted like the camp counselor/big brother he is, leading us through the airport into an awaiting Mercedes minibus that would take us into Manhattan to the London Hotel. I sat next to Alberto and felt his excitement. He was returning to the city where he had just graduated from college and was going to see old friends he hadn't seen in a while. Dom was texting with Matt Daddario, who was already at the hotel. Apparently there were many fans outside of the hotel dying to see them. The bus pulled up to a mob of fans waiting for them. As they stepped off posing for pictures and signing autographs, I felt like Brian Epstein with the Beatles. Darren and I strolled past and into the lobby, grinning from ear to ear. It was exciting. We had encountered this kind of thing with the Smallville cast at the San Diego Comic-Con, and it never got old.

The following day we met the Freeform publicity team in the lobby. We had worked with Catherine Graves and Amanda Pell before on Guilt and liked them both very much. They were kind and thoughtful. Catherine had set up an interview over breakfast with Jim Halterman, a TV critic from TV Guide. Jim was a big fan of the show and asked us a series of questions that we would hear again and again throughout the day. "How would our adaptation differ from the previous showrunner?" "What were our plans for season two?" "Did we feel intimidated by such a vocal and passionate fandom?" Jim recorded our conversation and was very encouraging, and before we knew it we were being led off to another van that drove us to the Hammersmith theater where the Shadowhunters panel was to take place. Darren and I rode in with Dom and his girlfriend at the time, Sarah Hyland, and Harry and his wife Shelby Rabara. I'm a big Modern Family fan so I was totally starstruck by Sarah, who couldn't have been sweeter. We arrived in the back of the theater and were led up a flight of steep stairs into the green room, where the rest of the cast waited to go on stage. Cassie arrived to speak on the panel, followed by McG in his red suit and cowboy hat - the consummate showman. The air was electric.

Catherine got everyone's attention and we followed her back down the stairs and into the darkness at the side of the stage. She lined everyone up in order of appearance and before we knew it the moderator, Adam Swift from TV Line, called my name. I stepped onto the stage into the glare of the blinding lights and the roar of applause, the audience full of screaming fans. Holy shit. This was crazy. They were screaming for this show that they loved with all their heart. The actors were introduced one by one and the crowd went even crazier. The moderator asked a few questions to the cast and us, and we answered as best as we could so as to not reveal any spoilers. McG did his thing, razzling and dazzling the crowd. And then the fans got their chance to come to the microphone and ask questions, and I got to meet the fandom in person for the first time. To say I was deeply moved would be an understatement. Listening to fan after fan tell Cassie how much these books have changed their lives -- how in some cases they had actually *saved* their lives -- gave me a lump in my throat and brought tears to my eyes. I realized then that this show was more than a television show. It was a platform to change lives. I left the stage exhilarated.

We were led into another van that drove us from the theater to the Javits center, where we would first have lunch and then do a series of press interviews. When we stepped off the van McG went to greet a line of fans and they went crazy, taking selfie after selfie with the rock star director. Catherine and her team ushered us into a room where we all ate sandwiches. I sat next to Sarah Hyland, and of course peppered her with questions about her show like any true fan. I heard about Harry's tour with Glee when they played the O2 arena in London. Isaiah mentioned he was working on preliminary plans to ask his girlfriend to marry him in New Zealand over the Christmas break. Kat was going to be back in New York to do press before the premiere right after the new year. Our quick conversations were gently interrupted by Catherine, ever the trooper as she led us toward the press room upstairs.

We were all to be paired up as we went from table to table to answer questions, a ten-minute limit for each session. At each table you sat across from three or four different reporters, all with audio and video recording devices. It was beyond intimidating for a guy like me who doesn't really edit himself very well and tends to go off on a tangent, especially when I'm excited. Darren and I were paired up with Cassie, who after seeing the premiere episode spoke very highly of the new direction of the show. Cassie was a total pro with the press, having done it so well with her books. I was more raw, as the videos on the internet can attest to. I made the mistake of using the term "ship" to describe a friendship rather than a romantic relationship. This led to a portion of the fandom believing that I was suggesting Clary and Isabelle were going to become lovers - not such a bad thing in some people's minds. This was the beginning of my steep learning curve thanks to the Shadowhunters fandom.

After an hour and a half, we were finished with our day. The cast was going off to do many more interviews, but for me and Darren, our Shadowhunters Comic-Con experience was over. While Darren went back to the hotel, I met my niece and nephew-in-law down on the main floor. My niece Samantha is very dear to me. I was a very involved uncle in her life until I had kids of my own. She had recently moved to New York with her then boyfriend, now husband, who was going to NYU law school. He was also a video-game loving fanboy who was in nirvana at his first Comic-Con. I warned them that the main floor was going to be crowded, and I wasn't lying. It was packed, but I had to stroll past the comic book stands for old times' sake. I collected comic books back when I was in fifth and sixth grade, only Marvel (because of the angst), and went to my first comic book convention with my grandmother where she bought me my gift for sixth grade graduation -- a copy of Daredevil Number One in fair to middling condition that I still cherish and which is proudly framed on my office wall.

The next morning, instead of flying home, I took a train down to Washington D.C. to visit my oldest daughter Maya who had just started college at the George Washington University. Because of the strain of starting Shadowhunters, I wasn't able to help move her into the dorms with my wife, so this would be the first time seeing her in her new habitat. On the train I took out my laptop and watched the director's cut for 204, headphones cranked as usual.

Like I always do, I watched it once without taking notes, and then ran it again and stopped intermittently as I made notes in a separate email. I then sent my thoughts to Darren and Zoe, who would compile our notes together and delete any overlapping thoughts. We would then look at notes from Matt Hastings and the writer of the episode to see which ones we supported and which ones we didn't. Once all the notes were stream-lined, we sent that document to the editor, assistant editor and the rest of the post team. After a few days they usually manage to implement all the notes and then send us another cut of the show. We either give another round of notes or come into the editing bay at that point and start to work on a more micro level on the episode. Once we're happy, we send it off to the powers that be and then do their notes. And so it goes, episode after episode until the season ends.

Some director's cuts receive minimum notes, but this cut for 204 felt off. Like 202, it didn't look as dark and moody as 201 and 203. I knew we could adjust when we color-timed the episode, but it was always better to capture the shadows and contrast when we were shooting. The cut was also edited by a newcomer to the show, so it was understandable that the pacing didn't exactly feel right. But the end. Oh my God. The end was phenomenal. The slow-motion aftermath touched me deeply. This was the sweet spot for the show. Operatic emotion set again beautiful cinema and sound. You didn't need words to understand when Simon rushes in and goes straight to Clary, staring into her empty gaze and realizing how devastated she is. Their embrace contrasted against the embrace of the Lightwood siblings was a powerful moment, and the song "Between the Wars" by Allman Brown was a beautiful soundtrack. This was when we began to realize how invaluable Lindsay Wolfington was to the show. It was confirmed in the next episode when she found another gem that would play over Jocelyn's funeral - "Don't Forget About Me" by Cloves. On the train I typed up all my notes and sent them off, then enjoyed a spectacular day with my daughter in Washington D.C. We had a delicious, special sushi lunch at a restaurant we heard Michelle Obama liked to frequent. I got to see her dorm room at last. And we toured the Lincoln Monument together, only mere blocks away from her dorm.

On the plane ride home that night I sat next to a woman who had three cell phones displayed in front of her. Ever the curious one, I struck up a conversation and learned that she was Judy Smith, the crisis control manager who the show SCANDAL was based on. We had an interesting conversation to say the least. Another perk of flying first class is you often sit next to interesting people. During my tenure on Shadowhunters, I spent three hours getting to know Gregg Sulkin, one of the stars of Marvel's RUNAWAYS, coming home from New York Comic-Con the following year. On one flight home from Toronto, while I was writing the sides for Jonathan Morgenstern's audition, the guy sitting next to me asked if I was writer. He looked familiar, and lo and behold it was Marc Blucas, the actor and former college basketball star who played at Wake Forest with NBA great Tim Duncan. I'm a huge basketball fan, and I peppered Marc with questions the whole ride home. I even read the "Jonathan" sides with him to see how it sounded aloud. If you ever find yourself sitting next to me on a plane, I promise I'll get to know you.

# A WINTER'S GROOVE

Back in Los Angeles my routine solidified as we moved forward through the season, no longer in a frantic rush to keep up but still always feeling like I'm up against the clock. A typical day involved time in the writer's room; time on my computer writing, answering emails, watching episode cuts; time in the post-production offices, whether it was editing a show, spotting or reviewing visual effect shots. Spotting sessions involve going through the show with our visual effects team and describing our ideas for the visual effects and where exactly we wanted them to go, frame by frame. When we arrived on the show the visual effects were being created and executed by a number of different vendors. The wolves were done by one house, and Magnus' magic was handled by another, the glamouring effect done by another, etc. We thought it would be more fluid if it all could be handled under one roof -- Folks VFX being the obvious choice. Based in Montreal, their work was amazing and one of their partners, Phillipe Thibault, had been on set during season two and was instrumental in helping Matt create the new look for the show. During our recent trip to Toronto I had spent a lot time with Phillipe and was convinced he was our guy. He was not only a brilliant artist with a creative mind, but he also lived in the practical world and was able to achieve undeniable greatness given the cost parameters. Spotting music and sound is the same idea. The showrunner goes through the episode scene by scene with the composer, music supervisor, sound team (over the phone in Toronto) and the editor manning the Avid, describing our thoughts to the team. I only went to the first few and then Darren took over from there while I usually used that time to be in the writer's room.

A writer's room is the brain of the show, usually filled with very smart people who, when functioning on all cylinders, spew out brilliant ideas that become artfully interwoven into a captivating story. When a room is grooving, it's like passing a ball to your teammates on a soccer or a basketball team, back and forth until you score a goal. It can be exhilarating, full of laughter and good times, and it can be deflating, full of empty white boards and headaches. When I began my career in TV, the writer's room was totally intimidating. We were story editors on season 2 of Smallville and I felt way over my head. Jeph Loeb, the guy who wrote Teen Wolf and Commando and was a huge comic book writer, was to my right. Mark Verheiden, who wrote The Mask, was on my left. Al Gough and Miles Millar were writing Spiderman 2. What the hell was I doing here? I was nowhere near as smart as these people. Eventually I found my groove and my time in the room became rewarding. Once I relaxed and "let the game come to me," I felt more comfortable. If you came up with an idea, it not only had to be good, but it needed to be pitched with passion and drama in order to sell its merit. I've always had pretty good verbal skills thanks to the genes passed on by my dad, and they paid off big time in this setting.

Once the room has created the story, each scene on a colored index card (color depending on if it's in the A, B or C story) taped up on a board, the story is verbally pitched to the showrunner. In OUR career the pitching was usually done by a Co-Executive Producer or Executive Producer who was in charge of the writer's room. But in the case of Shadowhunters, the writer of the episode was the one doing the pitching. Because we didn't want to mess with the mojo, we continued that process until season 3.

207 aka "How Art Thou Fallen" was essentially the second half of a two-parter in terms of the Cleophas story. Besides Valentine, Luke's sister would be the villain of the story until we paired her up with Clary and she underwent her crisis of conscience. Her involvement would give Luke the chance to play a part in the "A" story, something we had been wanting to do all season long. Valentine holding the angel Ithuriel captive and binding his wings felt especially brutal. It was a story from the books that I totally responded to, and this was a fine place for it. From the beginning of our career, Darren and I have always been intrigued by elderly characters with faces wrinkled with the lines of their long lives. We thought it would be cool to make the angel an old man while he was held captive, and then have him return to his younger self once he was healed. The story came together swiftly in the writer's room.

It was the ideal time for Jace to move into Magnus' apartment after getting kicked out of the Institute. It would complicate Alec's relationship with Magnus in the best way. I suggested Alec go to Izzy for advice with his love life. Many in the room thought I was crazy, but I thought it would be cute and endearing. Michael Reisz came up with one of my favorite lines in that scene when Izzy questions Alec about an old girlfriend -- "what about Jessica Blueheart?" Off Alec's guilty look, she then asks, "Was there even a Jessica Blueheart?" Hollie Overton delivered a really strong draft. Jace giving Simon pick-up tips in the Hunter's Moon made me laugh out loud when I read it. The line "dazzle me" was an instant classic. The scene with Luke and Cleophas at the Hunter's Moon was utterly heartbreaking, and Cleophas trying to redeem herself by helping Clary underscored the theme of sacrifice in the series.

The idea of Clary's visions came of course from the books, and it was an exciting challenge to tackle the adaptation and use the visions in the show. They began on our watch in 202, but those visions existed only to shake Jace out of his allegiance to Valentine. In 205 Clary saw the vision of the rune she was about to create. We knew we had to space these moments out and use them sparingly because their appearance carried the risk of being overly convenient, used only then the plot needs it. But the end of 207 screamed out for it, when she touched the angel Ithuriel. It would set up the idea that it was possible to destroy the Soul Sword in the finale. And it was a vision that Jace and Clary could share and interpret in different ways.

Ben Bray, a former stunt coordinator, was directing and brought a tremendous amount of energy and passion. Director of Photography Mike McMurray, shooting the odd episodes, was on board and we were thrilled. All of his episodes looked beautiful. Mike was particularly excited about the big action scene on the rooftop where Jace and Clary have to fend off Valentine's soldiers in order to free the angel. In the script it was written that it all was happening during a huge lightning storm, and Mike took that to heart in a big way, using a strobe effect to no end. When I saw the first cut it literally made my eyes hurt and my head throb. We had the editors snip out as much of the strobing as possible, but it was still intense. One of the producers wondered if it was even suitable for broadcast. In the end, after the visual effects were added and the color-timing done, it came out okay and forever earned Mike the playful nickname "Spanky McLightning", which Mike laughed about as much as everyone else. It was Mike's first and only odd choice in the thousands of hours of footage he shot for the show, which was always stellar.

After the episode aired, I was blindsided by the furious response from fans about Alec and Magnus' first sexual experience. Not only did they feel it was given short shrift and not enough screen time, but some fans were livid, claiming that Magnus didn't give Alec verbal consent when he led him into the bedroom. Their anger erupted over on Twitter, and they showered much of it on Hollie Overton, the writer of the episode. Poor Hollie had done nothing to warrant the criticism. She was following our directive, and I quickly took to Twitter to explain if they were angry they should be angry at me and Darren. And boy were they angry. Post after post chastised us for our poor decision making, and we both felt terrible about it. We had always wanted the scene to continue a little further, but for various production reasons we just didn't have the footage. The consent issue caused a bit of introspection as well. In the script and in the dailies, we felt that consent was clearly implied, but the fact that even a few fans felt it wasn't was enough to make us wonder. On the way to work the next day I imagined a future episode where we could flashback to that night and essentially "right our wrongs" by giving the audience the scenes that they missed. It would be beautiful and romantic. We agreed that as soon as we found the right episode for it, we'd deliver the moments these characters and this relationship deserved.

208 aka "Love is A Devil" was a show that had to be produced for a price. Since the first two episodes had been so over-budget, we had been slowly reducing our deficit as we went along, producing most of the shows under budget or right on budget with the idea that at the end of 210 we would be even. In the beginning of the season we quickly recognized that the young Unit Production Manager with a background in indie films was clearly bright, inspired and more than capable of taking over the reins. We promoted Chris Hatcher, and he became instrumental in helping us achieve cinematic greatness on a budget. There was nothing he wouldn't try to do, unlike many line producers whose first instinct is to say no. He and Matt Hastings worked as a team to bring the scripts to the screen and not break the bank, and they were clear that 208 needed to come in under. That would mean 7 days of shooting instead of the normal 8.

I've always liked the idea of having a party where all the characters could dress up, come together and interact with one another under one roof. And who better to throw that fabulous bash than an insecure Magnus Bane trying to impress Alec's Mother. I also loved the idea of bringing back little Max, Alec and Isabelle's younger brother, into the fold. He had yet to be seen in season two and the idea of him going through a bar mitzvah-like Shadowhunters ceremony where he received his first rune was awesome -- and cheap. The Isabelle and Raphael story also fit into our belt tightening mode and provided more insight into Raphael's character, which I yearned for. I loved his character in the book but felt the adaptation in season one leaned more into the character as a thuggish villain rather than a tortured, sensitive soul. The burgeoning relationship with Isabelle, dysfunctional yet beautiful at the same time, would give him more screen time and scenes that he could play with other characters besides Simon and Magnus.

After going through "the batting order", Shireen was back up to write

208. When I first heard the idea in the writer's room of a spell that made the characters hallucinate and have to face their worst fears, I was reluctant. It's a trope that every supernatural show seems to use. But the more we talked about it, the more I became convinced that it could be revealing and interesting at this point in the season considering what all the characters were going through, especially Alec. Iris Rouse being behind it all made it even more interesting, and the idea that as a warlock she could turn herself into a cat to get into the party and cast the spell from person to person was even better. We would set the cats up with a scene on Magnus' rooftop. Magnus was into cats in the book, and had a pet himself, but because Harry Shum is allergic, the pet cat idea was a nonstarter. But for one episode he was game, and it made sense that Magnus would act as a caretaker for all these neighborhood cats, feeding them milk. The Jace-Magnus scene on the rooftop is one of my favorites. Jace being a bit afraid of cats seemed like comic gold, and Jace warning Magnus to treat Alec well and not break his heart broke *my* heart.

The network was slightly hesitant about the idea of the spell. Up to this point the stories had pretty much sailed through the approval process. I would verbally pitch the show, followed by an outline written by the writer followed by the script, and production would begin. But for good reason, they recognized the trope and were worried it wasn't original enough. Darren and I assured them that through the Shadowhunters lens it would feel cool and fresh, and we got the green light to go to script. But after reading the initial script, we worried if we'd done enough to avoid the pitfalls of the concept. We dialed up the stakes and continued to tweak the story. Alec in his affected state being driven to possible suicide was a last-minute adjustment. It was certainly dramatic, and it made sense given his lingering, burning guilt over Jocelyn's death and fear that Clary will irrevocably hate him for it. I knew it would be controversial, but it fit the story so well that we decided to go for it. Knowing what I know now after it aired, I honestly don't think I would've written it that way. The last thing I want to do is create a trigger for someone, and after reading the Twitter reaction after it aired, it was clearly an issue for many people. The fans' reactions after the episode airings were often illuminating for me. I learned so much from them. My education was one of the greatest gifts of my experience in the shadow world.

We knew we wanted the party to have a theme. When Matt Hasting suggested a Spanish, flamenco vibe in prep, I was a tad worried it could feel cheesy. But when I heard that in the books Robert and Maryse had gotten engaged in Barcelona, it totally clicked. Magnus would throw the party for both of the parents not realizing they were having marital issues. Later in the episode we would pay that off in a heartbreaking scene where Maryse tells Jace and Alec of her husband's indiscretions. I cried from the moment I saw that scene and every time after. Nicola is absolutely brilliant. For the party we would have dancers and waiters, but we wouldn't go overboard with decorations. The music would help, and Lindsay ended up finding some great flamenco songs. Catriona McKenzie, an Australian director, did a great job grounding the performances, and her shotmaking was fluid and energetic. David Herrington's cinematography is among his best work on the show.

Post-production on the premiere and all that went along with it continued at a rapid rate. Launching season two required more than the episode. We wanted to replace the title sequence for season two with one that signaled a darker, more adult tone, and the network agreed as long as we could do it for a price. We shopped around for a bit and found a title house we all liked. Matt gathered the cast one by one on a green-screen stage with a massive wind fan and shot what you see in the credits today. We added Alisha of course in season three. We also worked on a recap for season one with the visual effects editor that would try and encapsulate all you needed to know if you had never watched the show before. Broadcast episodic recaps are often difficult because you have to jam in so much information in so little time, but summing up Shadowhunters season one while showing off as many cool visual effects as possible was especially tricky.

Usually when you mix a television show you go to a sound mixing stage where you watch the show on a larger screen and listen to it over huge speakers. For financial reasons, Shadowhunters was mixed and color-timed in Toronto. That meant we would participate remotely over a computer line. It wasn't something we had ever done before and it certainly wasn't optimal, but more and more shows are being done this way as production spreads all over the globe, and over time we got used to our trip to the 11th floor of the Freeform building in Burbank. It was a small, sound-proofed room that we made our home for 42 episodes, even more homey after I convinced the network to invest in a black-out curtain over the sliver of window so we could watch in total darkness. If not shooting, Matt was usually there in person in Toronto with our sound team - *Emmy winning and Academy Award nominated* sound team I should add. Our mixer Chris Cooke and sound editor Alex Bullick did the sound for Guillermo Del Toro's THE SHAPE OF WATER. We watched the show here in L.A. with our post supervisor Tommy and R.J. from the network manning the controls, jotting down our thoughts on notepads. When it was done, we hopped on the phone with Toronto and gave our thoughts. Because the picture was in sync, they would scroll to the moment we were talking about and adjust accordingly.

In Matt's director's cut for 201 he had used a lot of temp music cues from a Netflix show called MARCELLA, but now in the final mix they were replaced by the phenomenal score from Jack Wall and Trevor Morris. The music was mesmerizing and gave the show a sonic energy that fit so well with the new tone. It felt modern and classical all at once and helped underscore the emotion of every single scene. Because Trevor lives in Santa Barbara, Jack came to the episodic spotting sessions here in L.A., and spending time with him in the few spotting sessions I was in was always a pleasure. He understood the show deeply and his ideas were always spot on. As the show progressed, so did the musical palette. Their use of strings became more pronounced, and Jack's background in jazz came in handy during several scenes. Speaking of jazz, Magnus was a character that we felt would love music -- big band jazz in particular. We usually avoided using a popular song in Magnus scenes because he was so original, and it felt off for him to be listening to something from today considering he's lived all these hundreds of years. Of course, if we could have afforded a Queen or David Bowie song, we would've used them in a heartbeat.

Our coloring sessions also took place in that room until Season 2B, where we convinced the network that we needed to color-correct the show on a monitor and system built for the process and moved over to Technicolor. We were able to see the nuances much more clearly on any show, but particularly on a genre show creating new worlds and filled to the brim with visual effects, color correction was a crucial element. Whether it was Clary and Izzy's arrival in the marble grey land of the Iron Sisters, or the Oz-like splatters of color in the Seelie Court, we could either dial up or dial down what already existed on film. The golden, fiery hue in the City of Bones is a great example.

For the mix and coloring sessions, we liked to invite the writer of the episode if they were available. On Smallville, which we came up on, the showrunners hadn't involved writers in post-production at all. They weren't even asked to give notes on the cuts of their shows. After working on other shows and having some perspective, we realized that wasn't the best approach and vowed to involve the writer as much as possible. Though Darren and I are usually in sync with our taste, at times we can also have wildly different opinions, and bringing in a third party is often helpful in giving us some consensus. The writer's opinion in editing can be invaluable considering how intimate they've become with the material. On top of that, I enjoy mentoring talented writers, and exposing them to the post process only makes them better writers. Beginning on Smallville, I've always taken great joy in hiring and working with brilliant young writers and watching them soar. Many of them are now hugely successful writer/producers and showrunners, and their success feels like my own success. It has been one of the great pleasures of my career, as rewarding as watching a terrific episode of a show I helped make.

On a drizzly Sunday evening in mid-October, Darren and I drove out to the Hollywood Bowl to see Bon Iver, a band we both loved and who we had been listening to a lot of in the shadow world. I had purchased the tickets as a birthday present for him back in June, and the night was finally upon us. We knew Zoe was attending with her friends but in a crowd of fifteen thousand people I knew the odds we would see her were slim. Of course, when we were entering the venue who was directly beside us but Zoe and her sweet girlfriends. I was convinced there were no coincidences in the shadow world. It was Raziel's will.

Episode 209 aka "Bound by Blood", had a strong narrative drive coming off the last show when Iris Rouse told Clary she must find Madzie in order to repay the favor Clary owed her for bringing back her mom. It was organic and felt like we had planned it all in 205. Clary's rotting finger spreading across her body was admittedly not our finest hour, and I take the full blame. It felt like we needed stakes for the hunt, and Clary weakening and dying in the presence of her new boyfriend/best friend Simon and her brother (at the time) Jace felt like it could be emotional and at times funny. I loved Simon's adoration for Jace and Jace's total dismissal of Simon, and this was an opportunity to kind of flip it now that Simon was with Clary and Jace was on the outside looking in. Pete Binswanger aka the Simon whisperer was writing, and we were excited.

Isabelle getting closer to Raphael in their burgeoning co-dependent relationship fascinated me. Even though you knew the relationship was doomed in so many ways, I was somehow rooting for them. And the chemistry between the actors was electric. Raphael teaching Isabelle how to make tamales remains one of my favorite moments of the series. As soon as Pete pitched the idea, we all knew it was gold. Romantic and creepy at the same time, with the hot sauce looking like blood, it was Shadowhunters at its best, especially knowing that Alec was on the hunt to find her, and when he did, it wasn't going to be a happy reunion. The triangle between Alec, Magnus and Raphael was intriguing, and we wanted to exploit it while we could. Raphael was like Magnus's younger brother, and Alec wanted to kill him for what he was doing to his sister. Influenced by THE GODFATHER when Sonny Corleone (James Caan) barges in to rescue his sister (Talia Shire) from her abusive husband, I wanted Alec to clock Raphael across the jaw and try to bring home his sister, only to have Izzy, addicted to both yin fen and Raphael's charms, reject him and refuse to leave. It would be heartbreaking for Alec, Magnus and the audience, especially when Emeraude delivered such a powerful performance.

We knew we wanted to feature Maia in this episode. After having meaty scenes in 203 and 206, then a slight appearance as the bartender in 208, it was important to put her in the center of the story again instead of on the periphery. One of the frustrating issues of having eight lead characters is there isn't enough screen time in each episode to properly service each of them. Eventually we began experimenting with eliminating characters from episodes, but we quickly learned the fandom wasn't a big fan of that experiment. In 209 Maia mistakenly believes that Clary has the power to activate the soul sword and kill downworlders and takes it on herself to kill Clary before that happens. The wolf attack on Clary outside of the boat basin would be frightening, and then humiliating, when Maia is found behind the storage barrels, changed back into human form, naked and caught. Luke having to trap her inside the closet, knowing how claustrophobic she is, was a heart-wrenching example of parental tough love.

Our first downworld council meeting would be held in this episode, and give us an opportunity to bring back Meliorn, the Seelie Knight who had been scarred by the Queen for his forbidden relationship with Isabelle in season one. Because the show had been so crowded with cast, there had been no opportunity to include him in earlier episodes, but we were intrigued with the character from the outset and knew we wanted to use him from time to time. Matt Hastings, who directed 209, had our costume designer Shelley Mansell reconceptualize his wardrobe so he would appear more like a badass warrior. The scar along his cheek that the make-up team had expertly applied also added to the effect. When Matt first suggested holding the meeting at the Hunter's Moon, it felt awfully public, but the way he staged and shot the scene gave it the backroom mob vibe we were looking for.

Valentine and Madzie proved to be as amazing on film as they did on the page. Watching Valentine desperately trying to charm the powerful little warlock into doing his bidding is a pure pleasure. Alan Van Sprang is a terrific actor with enormous range - range we knew we wanted to explore as the season progressed. Madzie was a character who didn't need to speak much. Her actions spoke much louder than her words. The cafe scene when Madzie turns her hot cocoa into a fudgesicle is absolutely priceless. Matt Hastings had the idea of putting Valentine's hide-out in an abandoned carnival setting. It was a brilliant choice, not just because it was Valentine's naked attempt to try please little Madzie, but it was also creepy as hell. It was also a great place to have the episode climax with Simon getting kidnapped while he and Jace tried to save Clary.

As season 2a was coming into the final stretch, a few director openings became available in season 2b. Episode 216 was an open assignment, and the name Paul Wesley from THE VAMPIRE DIARIES was brought to our attention. We knew of Paul back when he was known as Paul Wasilewski and played Lex Luthor's younger brother Lucas in season 2 of Smallville. Paul was a big television star now with a giant following, and there was hope that his involvement in Shadowhunters could bring new viewers to the show. We knew that if he was acting on the show that would certainly be true, but we weren't so sure the same would apply to a project he took on as a director. He had helmed numerous episodes of Vampire Diaries, so we called Caroline Dries, a brilliant writer who we hired as an intern on Smallville so many years ago and who had risen to showrunner of Vampire Diaries in its later years, to get her opinion on his directing prowess. Caroline had nothing but great things to say about Paul as a director so we pulled the trigger. 218 was also open, and Matt Hastings was advocating for Amanda Row to fill that slot. Matt took great pleasure in championing his talented friends and colleagues, and he was integral in getting many of them hired. We often joked that he should open up his own management firm. But Amanda was more than that. She had been contributing creatively behind the scenes above and beyond being Matt's assistant, and Matt felt she was more than ready to helm an episode herself. We and the network were admittedly nervous about giving someone their first episodic directing gig on a show as complex as Shadowhunters. But Matt persisted. He promised us that her talent knew no bounds and he had no doubt she would crush her episode.We finally agreed to give Amanda a shot. It would be one of the smartest moves we'd make in the shadow world.

# THE BLANK PAGE

210 aka "By the Light of Dawn" would be the first script that we would write from scratch and have our names on. We were excited and intimidated all at once. To be directed by Joshua Butler, another Vampire Diaries/Originals alum that Matt Hastings had worked with before, the finale required scope on a reduced budget since we were still paying off the debts from earlier in the season. The episode also needed to wrap up various storylines while propelling new stories for the future. We would finally learn that Jace is in fact not Clary's brother, which would only complicate her burgeoning relationship with Simon moving forward. We also wanted to get a glimpse of Jonathan, our new villain for the rest of the series and a character that we wanted to introduce in the premiere of season 2B. Because we couldn't cast the actor so far ahead, we used a hidden Dom Sherwood in a hoodie to double as Jonathan.

I liked the idea of finally capturing Valentine at the end of the season and having him in the Institute as a prisoner for the first half of 2B. SILENCE OF THE LAMBS is one of my favorite films of its kind, and the notion of Valentine now being able to taunt Clary and Jace to their faces felt ripe with potential. The basement cells would also be a new set. The sword fight and subsequent face off between Valentine and Jace at the end of 210 was terrific because the Soul Sword was a great way for Jace to discover the truth about his relationship to Clary. And Luke the wolf bounding in to save Jace and take a knife wound from Valentine was a great heroic capper for our favorite Alpha.

One of the most exciting parts of adapting a book for film or television is coming up with new and exciting ways to bring the pages to the screen. When we took the job we knew we couldn't execute a literal adaptation. It would not only be cost prohibitive, but it would feel strange dramatically. In a book you can spend endless time in a character's head, reading their thoughts, but in a TV show or movie the drama usually needs to be expressed in some kind of narrative form. Also, as a fan of books and book adaptations, 1 always like when the writer takes risks and varies from the book in an unexpected way, but a way that fully captures the tone of its source material. Otherwise I find myself always ahead of the story, knowing what's going to happen next. How fun is that? Taylor Mallory became our go-to for everything and anything book related. Because she was a true book fan, her approval or disapproval meant a lot to us, and she approved of a lot in 210. Valentine holding Simon hostage and slicing open his neck to draw Clary out was a direct lift from the book, albeit in different circumstances. Simon feeding off of Clary was also from the book, but we added the twist that it was actually Jace, glamoured to look like Clary to gain entrance into the Institute. It would be Jace's angel blood that would turn Simon into a daylighter, an event that would not only cause major repercussions for Simon throughout season 2B, but also cause our crew to celebrate. The amount of night shoots would be greatly reduced now that our favorite vampire could hang out under the sun.

Raphael coming out as asexual was something we were all excited about bringing to the screen. Vampires had often been portrayed as sexual beings in film and television. The act of biting into one's skin and sucking their blood is interpreted as sexy by many. THE HUNGER, directed by Tony Scott and starring a young Susan Sarandon, Catherine Duneuve and David Bowie, is one my favorite vampire movies and one of the sexiest movies of all time. Raphael's asexuality was such an interesting side to his character considering how sexy David Castro came across with his deep voice and soulful stare. And because Isabelle had usually approached relationships with men in a sexual manner, his declaration would cause her to reevaluate her own priorities in a relationship. It was important for us to understand the intricacies and nuances of asexuality, and because as far as we knew no one on staff was asexual. Michael Reisz reached out to GLAAD, who gladly sent over a few "ace" individuals to discuss the topic with the staff. It was enlightening to say the least and helped us all understand Raphael's state of mind better.

The finale story for Malec needed to feel epic, and their first "I love you's" felt like the right fit. It just had to feel organic and earned. The idea that Magnus was in the Institute and could have died in the blast from the Soul Sword was something we wanted to milk for all it's worth. When you think you've lost someone forever, it can often lend clarity to how you really feel about that person. The idea that Magnus could be dead would torment Alec until he finally found Magnus and was able to hold him in his arms. And in that moment, getting back what he thought was gone, Alec would say the words he's never said before. It was a powerful moment on the page and Josh Butler brought it to life in a spectacularly moving way. Matt and Harry were at their best and the moment is one of my favorites.

Because Matt Hastings was directing 209, during the 210 prep I flew up to take the lead with Josh Butler for a few days, while Darren stayed back working on the continual flow of post-production and the season 2B break with the room. When I returned we would be pitching the broad strokes of 2B to the powers that be, a meeting that I was understandably anxious about. These next ten episodes would be the show we wanted to make, no longer bound by the previous regime's framework. It was like a fresh start and I was thrilled and terrified at the same time - my state of mind ninety-five percent of my waking hours. The core of my anxiety was the need to find the right actor to play Sebastian Verlac aka Jonathan Morgenstern. He was going to be the new big bad villain in 2B and the actor had to be vulnerable, scary, romantic and deranged all in one. Darren and I were each writing separate scenes for audition sides and we'd compare and tweak when I got back. Little did we know then that we would use those same scenes between

Valentine and Jonathan later in episode 216.

It was a chilly November evening in Toronto when I landed. This time I moved swiftly through customs and showed up at the hotel right on time for dinner with Kat. Kat had reached out to see if I had time to chat while I was up North, and because my days were packed with back to back meetings, I suggested dinner at the hotel. The Soho Met was the hotel of choice for many productions in Toronto, Shadowhunters included. All the visiting writers, directors and actors stayed here thanks to the discounted rate. But make no mistake about it. It's a lovely hotel located in the center of downtown, close to where most of the cast was living. Unfortunately, its signature restaurant is Dim Sum, which is great if you're in the mood for Dim Sum. Call me crazy, but I prefer my hotel food to be eclectic. Kat met me right on time, and over filet mignon rice bowls (the one non Dim Sum item in the place) we talked about all things Shadowhunters 2B. She was excited to hear about Sebastian's arrival and his obsession with Clary. The upcoming Seelie Court kiss made her squeal in delight. Kat was a huge book fan and loved nothing more than to see her favorite parts come to life on the show. She couldn't wait to trek to Alicante and fall into Lake Lyn. And the idea that Clary would raise the Angel Raziel to bring Jace back from the dead sent a shiver down her spine. She was pumped, and so was I.

The next morning I met Josh Butler in the production van headed from the hotel to the studio. Josh is a kind man with a treasure trove full of ideas. A former editor, he paid great attention to detail and after just a few hours with him I felt enormously confident. His questions and ideas about the script were spot on and he understood the material in a deep way. I visited the carnival set and met Madzie in person for the first time, as well as her sweet Mom. Dom was there in his black leather jacket, adorable with the little girl who constantly wanted to be held by him. Dom had heard about the new villain Jonathan Morgenstern we were planning to cast and had a friend he thought would be right for the role. He asked if he could send his friend's audition link directly to us instead of going through casting directors so we would be sure to see it. I of course said yes. This happened a lot on shows. Actors knew other actors and were often trying to get a friend on their show.

I gave Sir Hastings a hug of encouragement as he flitted about in full director mode. Pete Binswanger was hovering around video village, very much at home on set. The crew appeared to be in good spirits, looking forward to the upcoming winter break where they would have six weeks off before starting back up again in January. Of all the crew, the on-set personnel had the most grueling hours. The camera operators, grips, make-up and hair and other technicians worked thirteen and fourteen hour days every day. They didn't alternate episodes like the cinematographers or script supervisors. Production literally took over their lives.

The table read later that day went well. The actors were all in jovial moods, anticipating their Christmas break just like the crew. The supporting roles were all read by local actors who were sitting in on for the actors who couldn't make it. One of these actors was a young woman by the name of Sydney Meyer, who crushed every scene she read. Male, female, British accent, French accent, it didn't matter. You simply believed the words that came out of her mouth. We mentioned her obvious talent to Matt Hastings and told him we should find a role for her somewhere down the line. She was too good for her current job.

Upon returning to L.A., work on 2B continued in earnest. Darren and I sent out the sides for Jonathan to our casting directors and waited patiently. I spent as much time as I could in the writer's room helping map out the broad strokes of the upcoming season. The idea of Jonathan taking on the persona of Sebastian Verlac reminded me a lot of one of my favorite films, THE TALENTED MR. RIPLEY. Sebastian's plot goal was very clear to us from the start. He would ingratiate himself into the Institute so he could get close to his father and carry out his revenge, all while struggling with the romantic feelings he has for his dear sister Clary. It was twisted, that's for sure. We figured Valentine would be out of prison mid-season. He would talk his son out of killing him in the following episode, and then they would go on the hunt together for the remaining Mortal Instruments, culminating in Jonathan's death and Valentine raising the Angel Raziel. Isabelle would struggle with her addiction and overcome it in time to help her fellow Shadowhunters. Alec would become the new Head of the Institute, but it would cause a fissure in his relationship with Magnus that would threaten to tear them apart. Simon would deal with both the joys and horror of being a daylighter. Raphael and the other vampires would be desperate to find out how they can become daylighter themselves. Simon would also have to deal with the fateful kiss in the Seelie Court and the reality that Clary is in love with Jace. Luckily he would begin his relationship with Maia, a pairing we were all excited to write. Clary's vision and rune-making abilities would continue to grow, eventually leading her to Lake Lyn and her encounter with Raziel. After Valentine kills Jace, instead of Raziel killing Valentine like the books, I liked the idea of Clary being the one who kills her father. It would both strengthen and scar Clary on her hero's journey.

Luke's real-world job as a detective felt under-utilized in season 2a and we wanted to explore it more in 2b. Now that his poor partner Alaric was killed in 210, it made sense that he'd get a new partner. Knowing there was no sapphic representation on the show, I suggested making her a lesbian in a loving relationship with her partner. Michael Reisz coined the name "Ollie", short for Olivia, and we were off to the races. She would be constantly curious, always asking questions, which would make Luke's work life increasingly more difficult. Eventually it would climax at the end of the season when her curiosity causes her to show up at the Hunter's Moon wondering if Luke is a werewolf. We saw many decent auditions but none that blew away until we received a self-tape done in a make-up trailer by an actress named Alexandra Ordolis. She was our Ollie.

The season 2b pitch was held in a conference room at Freeform on a sunny November morning. I had my normal, anxious pit in my stomach as I waited in the lobby with Darren and Zoe, going over the beats in my head one last time. Zoe was there to take notes, and her enthusiasm and excitement about being in such a big meeting was inspiring. Margo Klewans and Robert Kulzer from Constantin arrived soon after, followed by Mary Viola with her trusted McDonald's iced tea in hand. We were led into a room where we met Jenn Gerstenblatt, Brian Lenard and Kirsten Creamer as well as Vanessa Aagaard from

Freeform casting. They were all very complimentary about the cuts they had seen and excited about the upcoming premiere in January. I started in on the pitch and fed off their reactions. It's always easier to pitch to people who respond to your ideas and these execs were there every step of the way. After it was over they shared a few thoughts but in general they were really pleased. We could begin writing 211. Darren and I walked back to the car, more than relieved. What we just pitched was truly our vision for the show and they loved it. We were finally settling in.

We returned to the office and filled in the writers, who were thrilled by the news. They had been used to struggling to get story approvals from the network, and this new harmony made their lives much easier. In our office we were greeted with an email from Dom Sherwood containing his friend Will Tudor's audition for Jonathan. Often times when an actor sends you a friend's audition it's a favor to their friend and the audition is just okay. But what we saw was not "just okay." It was remarkable. Shot in a tight close-up where his face filled the screen, it was the scene between he and Valentine where he recounts killing a man to conduct a physics experiment. He was vulnerable and terrifying. He was Jonathan. We quickly called Dom, who explained he met Will years ago when they worked together in a clothing shop in London, bonding over their acting auditions as they folded jeans. Will had been on GAME OF THRONES a few seasons ago and just finished a role on HUMANS. He and Dom now shared the same manager. We rushed downstairs to show the writers the audition and they all agreed. Will was fantastic. Matt Hastings seconded the motion and we sent the tape over to the network right away. Will Tudor was our first choice. Thank God they felt the same way.

211 aka "Mea Maxima Culpa" came together quickly in the writer's room. A lot of the ideas had already been generated during the molding of season two. Azazel was a greater demon from the books who was just the kind of formidable villain the premiere needed. Originally for his first appearance in the restaurant, we wanted Alec to be having a drink with Lydia Bramwell, his former fiancée now back in New York as part of the Inquisitor's security detail. She

would be supportive of Alec's blossoming relationship with Magnus, when suddenly Azazel appears and ends up killing Lydia among many others. It was a powerful moment on the page and immediately threw Alec into action. But Stephanie Bennet, the actress who plays Lydia, wasn't available. It was probably for the best. It was important that Alec be there for his parabatai in this show, and if Lydia died, it would've muddied his emotional direction.

The parabatai relationship between Jace and Alec was always something Darren and I, as lifelong friends, could relate to. 211 provided a terrific platform to explore this dynamic. The opening wrestling match between the two was playful but also poignant. Alec would use this occasion to try to get Jace to open up, albeit unsuccessfully. Later in the episode it felt like we needed a scene to bookend the first scene, where Jace would finally reveal his pained guilt to his parabatai. One night after work driving home, I envisioned a nonverbal scene where Alec would find Jace alone on the Institute rooftop, tears in his eyes. Their silent embrace was all that was needed to show that Alec understood Jace's pain and was there for him all the way. I quickly called Michael Reisz, the writer of the episode, and mentioned the idea. He shared my enthusiasm and added it to the script.

I was excited to bring back the Inquisitor, Imogen Herondale. Knowing how important she was in the books and how much her relationship with Jace would alter his journey, we knew she was going to play a big role in season 2b. In 211 we would reintroduce her by having her interrogate Valentine about the Mortal Instruments. It would help reset the mission to find the three artifacts and give her great scenes to play with Valentine. In all honesty, I wasn't a huge fan of The Inquisitor in season one. She felt over the top and I yearned to ground her more and make her feel more real. Matt and his team redesigned her wardrobe and hair and make-up to give her more stature and badassery. We also instructed Matt to direct her with more nuance and essentially dial down her performance. Mimi Kurzyk ended up blowing me away in this episode and all the others that followed. She was frightening and intimidating, but also maternal and thoughtful when she needed to be.

Azazel was a character we knew would anchor 211 and 212, which would end up being essentially a two-parter. Casting a greater demon who is all powerful can be tricky because you don't want them to be too over the top, but you also want to have fun. Early on in the conception of his character we all talked a lot about Frank Sinatra and the idea of this old school gentleman who loved New York City, 12-year-old Scotch, and killing a great deal of people with the flick of his finger. Brett Donahue's audition was good, but we had no idea how great he would be until we saw Matt's director's cut. He was charming and terrifying, and able to throw away the quips like they were blowing in the wind. After 212 we wanted to bring him back but could never find the right moment.

As production on season 2a wrapped up for the year, we huddled with Matt Hasting, production designer Doug McCullough and line producer Chris Hatcher to discuss the new sets we wanted to build for season 2b. On Smallville we learned the importance of introducing new characters and new sets every season in an attempt to keep the show as fresh as possible. Knowing we would be spending quite a bit of time in Sebastian's apartment, we needed to build that flat, as well as an adjoining closet to imprison the real Sebastian Verlac. A stove-top oven would be needed so he could conveniently burn his hand and cook his bouillabaisse soup. Knowing Valentine would be in captivity within the Institute, we wanted to build his cell as well as an adjoining area of hallways and crypts. Because winter was coming in Toronto, Matt made a push to add as much interior space that could be shot for outside at night, including several alleys as well as the outside of Hunter's Moon. With the help of visual effects backdrops and second unit New York texture shots, these locations often felt like they were outside when actually they were shot on the warmth of our stages. This not only saved money, but during the dead of winter it was greatly appreciated by the cast and crew.

# ALL HAIL THE BILLBOARDS

The billboards began appearing throughout Los Angeles with the cool, new black and white key art for season 2, the only colors present the red in Clary's hair and the gold in Magnus' cat eyes. The marketing department had done a terrific job rebranding the new mature tone of the show. A few of the billboards were close to our homes, and Darren and I got a kick out of seeing them. If we were ever feeling burnt out, the billboards immediately energized us. We replaced the season one poster in our office with the new art, a symbol of us taking ownership of the show.

Because 201 was going to air over the winter break, Darren and I decided to throw a holiday party for the crew in Los Angeles to show our appreciation before everyone disappeared on holiday. We anointed Zoe as our party planner, a job she gracefully performed while juggling her normal duties. While production was on hiatus in Toronto, post-production continued its blistering pace here in L.A. To make the schedule work, 210 was due to be delivered to the network right before the holiday break. The goal for the writer's room was to have the scripts finished for 211 and 212 while the 213 script and 214 outline would be written over the break. It would be a busy December.

Bryan Q Miller's deal was finally closing. He would come aboard after the new year working part time as a consulting producer. If we received a season 3 he would move up to co-executive producer. We knew the staff would feel anxious by his arrival and interpret it as a lack of satisfaction in their work, but nothing could have been farther from the truth. They were continually coming up with great ideas and cooking up great stories. The truth was that Q not only had the perfect sensibility for Shadowhunters, but he knew our taste inside and out. We had already worked with him on four shows and we had a natural shorthand with him. But we were sensitive to their reaction and didn't want to create any sort of distraction in the middle of an extremely busy time. So we decided to wait until their last day to break the news.

One of the worst parts of being a showrunner is the difficult conversations you are forced to have with creative people when you don't respond to the endeavor that they've put their heart and soul into for who knows how many hours of their precious lives. Whether it be a writer, editor, production designer, costume designer, director, actor, etc, as a showrunner you sometimes find yourself at odds with their vision and have to communicate that, even if it means causing disappointment and hurt feelings. As a writer on a staff, I know what it's like to turn in a script and have my showrunner ask another writer in the office next to ours to completely rewrite the script, without saying a word to me and Darren. Avoidance is a common way many showrunners deal with disappointment over a script or cut. They simply avoid talking to that person. Once we suffered through that as writers, we vowed to always be transparent with our staff and tell them how we honestly feel. Sure, this might hurt people and ruffle feathers, but as long as we were direct in telling our truth, we knew we were doing the right thing.

As Michael Reisz went off to write the outline for 211, the room began working on 212 aka "You Are Not Your Own." The idea of Valentine and Magnus switching bodies at the hands of Azazel was something Darren and I brought to the table. We had written an episode of Smallville back in season 4 called

"Transference" that was similar in its basic concept -- a character locked in prison switches bodies with someone on the outside as a means to escape. Valentine and Magnus were such disparate characters with completely polar opposite points of view that their body switching would be a delicious joy to experience. The network didn't exactly feel the same way. We received a call from Brian and Kirsten in my car on our way to a sound mix. They were worried the episode would be too cheesy and the comedy of it all would outweigh the gravity of the situation. I assured them it would not be cheesy. Yes, it would be darkly comical at times, but in the end it would be horrifying. Magnus having to sit in that cell in a straitjacket awaiting execution would be nightmarish to say the least. And Valentine trying to act like Magnus would be comedic but also terrifying when he was pleading with Alec to believe him. Harry Shum and Alan Van Sprang were thrilled by the idea and couldn't wait to get in front of the camera. We suggested they each try to come to the other's scenes in the beginning of the shoot to watch each other's actions and mannerisms in order to try and duplicate them in a way that would feel honest and real, and they were more than game.

The story break of a body-switching episode can drive a writer's room crazy when the logic gets to be too much of a barrier. I recognized this was happening here. Jamie Gorenberg, the wonderful writer of this episode, is a woman of logic through and through. When she suggested branching off by herself to work out the rest of the story, allowing the room to move on to 213, we thought it was a great idea. Jamie went up into her office next to ours and worked her magic, putting up cards up on her corkboard. I spent a morning working with her, moving around cards, suggesting tweaks, but I could feel something special was brewing. And the script did not disappoint. It was fantastic. Jamie had fully bought into the shadow world and her words brought the story to life in magical ways. We were blown away, and the network finally understood what we were going for. When we saw Billie Woodruff's director's cut, we immediately knew this show was going to be a perennial fan favorite. Alan Van Sprang as Magnus pleading with Alec to believe him gives me goosebumps every time I watch it. Harry's use of his body and hand movements to mimic Valentine is staggeringly accurate, and both of their performances ground the show in a real way. Throw in Will Tudor as Sebastian urging Clary to use her pain in order to create a rune, and Simon and Izzy together with his Aunt Rosario who tells them they make a cute couple, and the episode is one of my favorites.

Early one December morning Tommy Summers, our post producer, came to see us in our office. We knew the job was becoming an increasing strain on his life and we weren't shocked when he announced his resignation. Tommy has three young boys of his own and had recently adopted his sister-in-law's young baby and toddler as well. If you believe there are angels walking among us, Tommy is living proof. He never complained once during our time with him, but we knew the pressure had to weigh on him. He graciously offered to stay until the holiday break while we looked for his replacement. I gave him a long hug and told him he was a good man. There would be millions of jobs ahead of him but now he had to be there for his family.

The network sent over several resumes and we interviewed two people. Marc Kahn had been on CASTLE for its entire run and had just returned from a long holiday in Greece. Well rested with a perpetual smile on his face, Marc impressed us immediately. While he had never done a show before with this amount of action and visual effects, he had a natural ease and confidence that put our worries to rest. One of the most important facets of the job of a post-production producer is making sure there is a proper internal workflow so that the shows can be delivered to the network on time. Because Shadowhunters had to be delivered to two networks, Freeform and Netflix, with two different delivery requirements, the job was even trickier. Marc brought in his own support staff, then immediately secured us a deal with Technicolor so that we could color-correct the remaining episodes on a proper monitor. He quickly developed a strong relationship with our new visual effects producer, Folks, which would continue over time and helped shape the ease of posting each episode. He would fly to Toronto with us in January to meet the sound team and the new colorist in person. To this day Marc remains one of the best hires we've ever made, and a producer we plan on working with again and again.

Episode 213 aka "Those with Demon Blood" (aptly titled by Darren) would be the most political show of the entire series, in large part the result of the disastrous Presidential elections that devastated our entire staff, including myself. The night of the election was completely surreal for all of us. I had assumed, as did millions of Americans, that Donald Trump was unelectable. After the Access Hollywood tape was leaked where he could be seen and heard boasting about his various sexual assaults, I was sure no one, no matter what political party they belonged to, would ever vote for this man. But I was wrong. Tragically wrong.

The morning after the election I flew out to Toronto to help prep 210 in a total fog. It felt surreal to be in another country where people appeared to be totally unaware of the nightmare that unfolded the night before. Of course, the exception had to be the driver who picked me up at the airport, a female transport driver who I had actually met on Defiance. She had always been friendly, but this evening she chose the wrong time to espouse her conservative political views. As she ranted on about the immigration problem in Canada, I felt my muscles tighten to the point that I was literally clenching my jaw in order to stop myself from responding. I pride myself on being friendly to every single person on the crew, no matter what their title is. A driver, an actor, a caterer, an extra. It made no difference to me. I want everyone to feel welcome and appreciated for the work they do on our show. But at this particular moment, I couldn't help myself. I asked her to please stop talking.

The idea of downworld oppression existed throughout the books and felt particularly relevant to the real world after the election. To me, "the downworld" was synonymous with all of us who feel different and alienated from the societal norms that seem to box us in to behave in a certain way. It was certainly the theme that struck the biggest chord in me and was vital in drawing me into the shadow world. This episode was a chance to reflect on our new government's desire to suppress those that were different. The episode felt unusually important to us, and I think all the writers felt it in their post-election malaise.

Jace's accidental slaughter of those downworlders charging the Institute in 210 was an event we knew would have massive repercussions for many episodes to come. The downworlders' desire to destroy the Soul Sword so that kind of atrocity could never happen again would go unfulfilled thanks to the Clave conspiracy to keep its disappearance quiet. This would create anger and distrust among the downworlders, and it could very well lead to some kind of retaliation against the Shadowhunters. And thus began the central core idea to the episode. Darren and I have never been fans of police procedurals. We both appreciated their clever twists and turns but were more drawn to stories where the plot took a backseat to character driven moments. But this episode felt ripe for a good old fashioned, hard boiled murder mystery that would enable us to weave in the themes of racism and oppression without being overly preachy. There would be various suspects and a Clave investigation, and hopefully when you eventually discovered who the killer was you would be genuinely surprised.

The episode also provided an opportunity to finally showcase the music of Simon Lewis, something we had been looking forward to ever since we began working on the show. The network warned us from the beginning they were concerned that Simon playing music on the show could come off as cheesy. But we guaranteed them it would be the opposite of mozzarella and provolone. It would be entertaining and enlightening, a chance to see a whole different side of the nerdy Simon Lewis, and most importantly, it wouldn't feel stuck in. It would feel earned. And in this particular episode, after all Simon had been through, it felt right that Simon would pen an original song about the state of the downworld. So we turned to our new friend Sam Hollander to write and produce a song especially for the occasion. He called it "Fragile World" and when we heard that first demo we were blown away. The lyrics were spot-on, and the music was exactly what we had in mind. Alberto would go into a recording studio in Toronto before we shot the performance and pre-record his vocal, and then we would play the song back during filming. Alberto crushed his vocals in the studio, and his performance in the Hunter's Moon at the end of the show felt totally authentic.

Before we began working on 211, Darren and I created our "writers' batting order" for season 2B, and Zac Hug was scheduled to write 213. Numerous factors go into making that order. We tend to keep the writers who are integral to the success of the writer's room in that room as long as possible. In our world the Co-EP - our number two - usually writes their episode at the end of the season because we need them in the room leading the charge. It has nothing to do with matching a writer's strength to the actual material because we never know what the next episode is going to be until we're working on that episode. We also like to give the writer an early heads up to help them navigate their personal lives around writing a script. Zac had a great quirky sense of humor that played extremely well in his last episode. 213 aka Those with Demon Blood would be one of the most serious episodes of the series, and Zac was up for the challenge. Of course, it wouldn't be a Zac Hug episode without a bit of comic flair. I was obsessed with the notion that Magnus had been close with Freddie Mercury over the years. It felt so right. Leave it to Zac to write the line where Dot acknowledged their affair, claiming with a smile, "we will rock you indeed."

We knew there would be repercussions between Alec and Magnus after the events of 212. When your boyfriend is trapped in someone else's villainous body and pleads with you to save them, and you don't believe them, it's going to be strange afterwards. We amplified their discord by having Alec ask Magnus for a strand of his hair to check his DNA in a blatant display of downworld profiling. This would result in their first "fight" as a couple, which we knew would anger the many fans who wanted nothing but bliss between these two characters but would act as an obstacle they had to overcome. I loved the idea of bringing Dot back into the story and revealing that she and Magnus used to be a couple, a comfortable couple, two warlocks in love.

As their drinking and flirting increased, the idea of she and Magnus sharing a dance with a tad of magic thrown in thrilled me to no end. We had wanted to take advantage of Harry's dancing and choreography skills from the day we started, and this dance with Dot was the opportunity. We hopped on the phone with Harry and explained what we were thinking - a big band musical vibe, something uptempo that would showcase his moves. Our music supervisor Lindsay found a song we liked, and we sent it over to Harry to work his magic. Days later we received a video recorded in Harry's Toronto apartment with he and Vanessa Matsui dancing their hearts out. It blew us away. The choreography and vibe were exactly what we envisioned.

Michael Goi was scheduled to direct. Primarily a cinematographer known for his innovative work on AMERICAN HORROR STORY, Michael was smart but subdued, and we wondered about his ability to work with the cast. But when we saw his director's cut, the performances were all strong. Alberto and Alisha, who were at the heart of the story, delivered heartfelt performances in every scene. After the table read, Alisha called me to ask if she could tweak a line, the one in which she says she'd been called out being black before by the police, but she thought the shadowhunters were above that. I loved it right away. Because I was alone in my car, I told her I'd talk to Darren to see if he was down. We usually shied away from any overt connection to the real world because we recognized early on that the show acted as pure escapism for much of the audience - a chance to lose themselves in 42 minutes of entertainment without running the risk of being reminded of the stress of their real lives. But this felt relevant in a cool, shadow world kind of way. Darren wholeheartedly agreed.

Ironically, the cinematography in that episode, specifically the abundance of Dutch angles (titled frames) and the 360-tracking shot around Simon and the vampires, drove me absolutely crazy. I love visual flair and the use of cinematic style as much as anyone, but only when it supports the storytelling. The visual flair in this episode continually takes me out of the story when it should be invisible to the audience, too caught up in the story to notice. An example is the camera drifting away from Magnus and Alec kissing. We knew it would infuriate our audience, but it was all done in one shot, so we had no options in the editing room.

The holiday party was a welcome distraction from the end of the year crunch. We found a quaint wine bar nearby and Zoe deftly handled the party planning. It was wine, beer and hor 'd'oeuvres from 6-8. I had slaved over the creation of a music playlist using songs from the show and Zoe left early to set it all up. On a chilly Wednesday evening, all the writers got dressed up and went over to the restaurant, where the L.A. crew finally got the chance to hang out together. Post-production and the writer's room, while physically close by, remained each in a separate universe, rarely crossing with each other. A party like this enabled all of them to hang out and get to know one another. In addition, our friends from Constantin Films and the network joined us, as well as Mary Viola. The cast that was in Los Angeles all showed up. Kat was there, full of her usual grace and charm. Dom arrived with Sarah Hyland. Harry was there with his fiancée Shelby and manager. Isaiah showed up in good cheer, and I couldn't help but let him know that the beginnings of a Luke/Maryse romance was on the horizon. Isaiah loved the idea. The party was crowded and the energy was positive. As is my custom, I left early, a smile on my face as I acknowledged this idea of throwing a holiday party was definitely a good one.

# THE HOME STRETCH

With just only a little time left before our three-week holiday break, we dug down deep with the writers to try and finish a beat sheet so the writer of the episode could write the outline over vacation. Because writing over a holiday break can often suck, the task is usually based on seniority and a junior member of the staff normally becomes the chosen one. In this case, in our batting order, we anointed it as the freelance episode to be written by our writer's assistant, Taylor Mallory aka TMI fangirl like no other. Taylor had impressed us the day we started on the show. Not only was she an expert on all things book related, but her ideas in the room were all smart and solid, especially her dialog pitches when the writers evaluated the table reads. Because she was such a book fan, it was coincidental perfection that she would be the one to write the show's introduction to the Seelie Queen and the beloved book scene where Clary is forced to kiss the one she truly loves.

While I knew how important that scene was to the millions of book fans across the globe, I must admit I struggled with it. It all felt so silly and childish coming from this grown Queen. And then it hit me one morning in the writer's room. What if the Queen appeared as a child? What if she could manipulate her age to whatever age was better suited to the situation she was in. By posing as a young girl the first time they met her, she would come off as innocent and non-threatening as a way to earn their trust, especially the daylighter Simon Lewis. It would be weird and creepy in the best way, and give us permission in future episodes to cast whatever actress fits the part based on the Queen's mood. How awesome. Not everyone was down with it. Some worried diehard book fans would take umbrage. But I thought book fans would find the twist entertaining and unexpected. The network was concerned about finding a young actress good enough to pull it off, but I assured them we'd find a gem. There were talented child actors out there. Young Arianna Williams who played Madzie might not win an Oscar anytime soon, but they saw how successful that casting turned out to be. They trusted us, and we found the gem that is Lola Flanery.

One of the primary reasons we chose a Seelie to be the killer in 213 was because it would provide a logical reason for Clary, Jace and Simon to trek to the Seelie Queen in the following episode. It was a Clave murder investigation, which would give a sense of urgency to the journey. That storyline came about quite easily since the books had already outlined the foundation. Now that Alec was in charge of the Institute, he would create the Downworld Council as a way of trying to reach out and assuage the friction with the Shadowhunters. This would allow Magnus, Luke, Raphael, and Meliorn to be together in the same scene with Alec and Izzy, and the tension would be palpable. Add Sebastian to the mix and it would be even more tantalizing. I saw how much Will Tudor and Sebastian's character elevated the show in 211 and 212, and I was thrilled to have him back in the show after he sat out 213. When we hired Will for season 2B it was with the understanding we would use him in seven out of the ten episodes, but we quickly realized he shouldn't sit out again. He was terrific in every scene he was in. There wasn't a single moment when his performance didn't feel absolutely authentic.

I had wanted to see Jace playing piano since we started on the show, and this episode felt like when it would happen. It was also an opportunity to see the beginnings of Sebastian's obsession/hate over Jace Herondale and would be a nice bookend to the episode. In the first scene Sebastian watches Jace playing, and then in the last scene he eerily copies Jace's playing note for note on his own piano, all while the real Sebastian Verlac lies tied up in the closet.

The film PHONE BOOTH starring Colin Farrel and the voice of Keifer Sutherland was a movie that I thoroughly enjoyed. That concept of having an indistinguishable voice on the other end of a phone manipulating your every move was the inspiration for Sebastian's disguised voice manipulating Luke. It felt like a clever way to have Sebastian in the show without giving away that he was behind it all. One could say that Luke was pretty stupid and naive to trust this unidentifiable voice instructing him how to get inside the sub cells to kill Valentine, but I felt Luke was emotionally worked up enough to go with it. It was a cool complication and fit the story well.

The Thursday before the break we were summoned down to the writer's room to hear the full pitch for 214. We had made it a point to be in the writer's room as much as possible since we began on the show. We clearly had different story-telling instincts than the previous showrunner, so by listening to our ideas and our reaction to their ideas, the writers would gradually learn our taste. As post-production consumed us, our time was more limited in the room, but by 214 it felt like the writers were more in sync than ever, and the pitch to 214 did not disappoint. As was the custom on this show, the writer of the episode pitched their story. This was unusual for me and Darren. We were used to the Co-EP, our number two, pitching us the story on behalf of the room. This took pressure off the episode writer and guaranteed us a strong pitch because of the Co-EP's proven pitching abilities. Being a great writer doesn't necessarily mean you have strong verbal skills, but in television those skills are vitally important. Taylor was a theater arts kid and completely at home standing at the white board telling us the story. And as a fan girl who held this book series so close to her heart, her excitement was totally infectious. I was completely captivated, and after we made a few suggestions here and there, we gave her the green light to begin work on the outline.

Taylor's outline was strong, and her script even stronger. One lowers their expectations when evaluating a freelancer's work, but Taylor knew the show better than anyone and the moments were all there on the page. Simon, Jace and Clary musing about middle school. Ollie telling Luke to "use protection. And I don't mean your gun". The Queen telling Simon she worked with Sia and Bjork was a Slavkin-Swimmer touch, but all the other Seelie Queen dialog was Taylor all the way. Her talent was obvious, and I knew right away if there was a season three, she'd be on the writing staff.

214 aka "The Fair Folk" is one of my favorite episodes of the series. Not only is the story and script particularly strong, but director Chris Grismer delivered the best looking and best performed show up to now. Chris was scheduled to shoot episode 213, but with both scripts completed, Matt Hastings suggested we shoot the scripts out of order and have Chris shoot 214. Matt had worked with Chris before and knew he had the skills and talent to build a world like the Seelie realm. With help from Doug McCullough's art department and our friends at Folks Vfx, Chris created a Seelie Court that surpassed all of my expectations. His Seelie Forest was also a visual feast, bright flowers dotting the grey, snowy landscape. During the coloring of the show, Darren and I dialed up those flowers to a technicolor ten. Matt Hastings, who sat in on the sessions in Toronto, warned us that it felt too bright, but we were intent on bringing The Wizard of Oz to the shadow world. We rarely had differing opinions with Matt on visual style, but here we were at a standstill. Ever the gentleman, Matt conceded. Of course, when the network saw the cut, their first note was that the color of the flowers in the Seelie forest was too bright. Ouch. We were wrong. He was right. Live and learn.

The visual effects in the episode were mind blowing. The falling snowflakes looked utterly realistic. The flowing stream of water under the bridge in Central Park was a complete visual effect creation. Mike McMurray's cinematography is exquisite throughout, every shot deftly directed by Grismer's sure hand. The performances are all spot on, not a false beat in the entire show. Maryse and Isabelle's conversation at the end of the show tears me up every time.

Clary banging on the boathouse door for Simon to let her in only silenced by his loud, angry power chord is the kind of operatic Shadowhunters moment I live for, only topped off by the beautiful embrace shared by Clary and Izzy, both devastated by their respective heartbreaks. Isaiah Mustafa was at the top of his game as he had been all season long. Luke's anger toward Valentine was palpable. Our new editor, Karen Castaneda, cut the show and it felt like she had been with us from the beginning. Her taste and pacing were impeccable. Much like I felt after I watched 205, I realized the show was getting better and better.

The Friday before our holiday break, we gathered everyone into the writer's room to break the news that Bryan "Q" Miller would be joining us on the Monday after the break as a consulting producer working part time. I could feel the tension rise and assured them that his appearance had nothing to do with their abilities. They had all been doing extraordinary work. Q was a writer who we had hired on our last 4 shows and had proven to be a tremendous asset on every one of them. He was also a comic book scribe who lived and breathed genre material like Shadowhuunters. We told them they had been extremely welcoming toward us during a difficult time where their beloved former boss and leader had been replaced by strangers, and we appreciated that more than they knew. They all smiled and nodded but I could feel the unease that had suddenly crept into the room. We hoped that once they met Q and spent time with the guy, any trepidation they might have had about a newcomer joining the fray would go away.

More personnel decisions had to be sorted out before we left for holiday. Marc Kahn, our new post producer, was bringing in a few people he had worked with before, as is the custom with these gigs. That meant some folks under the previous regime had to be replaced. We also made the tough decision to replace another editor. These decisions and conversations are never easy. People's livelihoods are on the line. But in the end we were hired to do what we believe is best for the show, and we knew these decisions would make the show better. That last day of the working year we turned in our network cut for 210. The new post-production regime would begin in earnest on season 2b, and those episodes speak for themselves as to the undeniable talent of Marc Kahn and his team. All television series rely on post-production to improve and enhance the show, but Shadowhunters post takes it to another. The editing is superb. The level of visual effects, in both quantity and quality, is sky high in almost every episode. The epic musical score and emotional songs create a unique soundscape wonderfully mixed and designed. Add the brilliant coloring done on every episode and the impact is enormous.

# HOLIDAY IN THE SHADOW WORLD

The break was certainly relaxing, but the show was never out of mind for very long. I now had the time to deep dive into the books and continue to read as much as I could while also reviewing and giving notes on the script for 213 and the outline for 214. The script for 211 was baked like a delicious tray of chocolate chip cookies, but we were still waiting for Sir Hastings to taste it. Matt had just had a baby girl in early December and was out in Los Angeles with his family enjoying the bliss in his beautiful canyon home. He was due to direct episode 211 when production resumed in mid-January and we were anxious to get his feedback so we could tweak the script accordingly. Reading a Shadowhunters script wasn't exactly his priority at the moment, which we completely understood. He had a newborn and a two-year-old son. I am a total baby person, and I was anxious to meet his baby girl as soon as I could. One late December afternoon I made the trek up to Nichols Canyon, passing a huge Shadowhunters billboard at Sunset and La Brea on my way. We laughed about it at his home over a glass of Rose. We both felt enormously fortunate and overwhelmed with a sense of thrilling anticipation. Finally the world would see our collective work, and hopefully wouldn't think it sucked compared to season one. After playing with his baby boy and gazing at his sleeping baby girl, I made my way out, gently reminding him how excited I was to hear his thoughts about 211. It was a script we were really proud of.

Over New Year's my wife and younger daughter Cameron and I travelled to New York City to have a proper vacation away from it all. My older daughter Maya was on a Birthright trip to Israel and would join us a few days later. We stayed at a hotel in the heart of Gossip Girl land, which my daughter was obsessed with at the time. We walked and gawked. We ate delicious food. And we saw Dear Evan Hansen on Broadway, which completely broke me. Weeks earlier in the writer's room when we talked about our plans for the break and I mentioned I was going to New York, Hollie Overton urged me to see this play. She was a theater geek, and her love for this production was palpable. I tried to get tickets, but it was sold out. Sold out as in even my agents at WME couldn't score a seat. Days later I was playing tennis with Jonathan Caren, an uber-talented playwright/TV writer who we had hired on our Melrose Place reboot years ago. When I told him I was headed to New York and in search of a Broadway experience, he of course brought up Dear Evan Hansen. I told him I knew all about it but sadly it was sold out. He said he was close with the associate director and offered to make a call. Not only did he come through, but luckily she could only get a pair and a single. Meaning I was sitting alone, in the sixth row, where my teenage daughter couldn't witness my uncontrollable sobbing. For the record, I was particularly emotionally raw at the moment. A week and a half earlier, the brother of a dear friend of mine committed suicide. He was someone I had met when I was fourteen years old. I had just gone to his funeral. It was the fourth funeral of a friend who had committed suicide in the last four years. I was numb, and this play was my release.

As much as I wanted to have a small respite from the shadow world in order to clear my head, the amazing juggernaut that is Freeform marketing wouldn't hear of it. Those first two days of January, Shadowhunters posters seemed to be plastered everywhere throughout Manhattan, from Subway platforms to a Times Square digital billboard. I hadn't been bombarded with billboards from I show I had worked on since Melrose Place, where it seemed you couldn't go anywhere in Los Angeles without seeing them. It is always a goosebump-inducing moment.

The day of the premiere we found ourselves in Soho, bundled up against the winter chill as we navigated our way through a parade of shops, galleries, bookstores and bakeries. It was a beautiful day where I continually checked my watch, making sure I had enough time to travel back to my hotel room on the upper east side by eight o'clock, where I could sit in front of the TV with enough time to find the Freeform channel and get a firm handle on my Twitter feed to observe the reaction firsthand. How surreal it was to race down the stairs of a subway station in Soho to watch your show and rush by a Magnus billboard. It was one of those special moments that you know is special when it's actually happening.

I had live tweeted for shows in the past and the fan reaction was always inspiring, but it was always only a small number of people. I knew the Shadowhunters social media was enormous, but I had no idea how enormous it was until the show began. It felt like hundreds of fans were commenting on every single second of the episode. I had never watched television this way, let alone television that I was intimately involved with. It was deeply rewarding and only slightly hurtful. While most of the reactions were positive, some were negative (to put it mildly), yet often deeply instructive. No one knew the material better than the fans, and we were completely cognizant of the fact that we were brand new to this richly inhabited, deeply complex, mythological world that hardcore book fans knew a lot better than we did at this point. Of course, our own reading and the veteran writing staff were helping us improve daily, but the fan reaction and interaction certainly helped as well.

The Twitter reactions didn't stop once the show ended. In fact, it felt like it was building. I was flooded with questions from bright and eager fans and I began to answer when I could. This was when my relationship with the Twitter shadow family truly began. We were only flirting until then but now we were seriously involved. Because the show premiered 10 hours later on Netflix throughout the rest of the world, the reaction was even bigger the following day. It was a Twitter party in the shadow world twenty-four seven, chalk full of pics, gifs, videos and artwork created by fans who clearly had enormous talent. It felt like I was getting injections of inspiration every time I turned on my Twitter feed. Never before had I felt so connected to an audience. Back in the day when I was working on Smallville, the audience was loyal and passionate, but that was before the days of Twitter. I could only see their reactions on the various message boards connected to fan sites or when I met them in person at Comic-Cons. The Shadowhunters fan experience was entirely different and deeply gratifying on a whole other level.

The following day, my wife, daughter and I walked across the Brooklyn Bridge to spend some time in the hip, happening borough before meeting my niece and her fiancé for dinner after they got off work. As we meandered through shops and more bakeries, I nervously checked my phone for news of the ratings for the premiere. In America, the success of broadcast television shows used to be based entirely on live ratings. Today the metric has changed to include Live-plus-3-days and Live-plus-7-days to account for the viewer who has recorded the show and watched it within a certain period of time. It doesn't account for those who view the show on their computer using streaming apps. That's a whole different system. Freeform had been promoting their streaming app at the time and wanted people to watch over their platform; however, they were still broadcasting the show on cable television, and those ratings helped determine how much money the network would receive from advertisers. I knew those live ratings mattered, and I was anxious to say the least about how the show performed.

While eating lunch in a mouth-watering taqueria, I received a call on my cell phone with the recognizable number of our trusted network executives Brian and Kirsten. It was early in Los Angeles for ratings news, but often the network receives the ratings before the press. Darren was anxiously waiting on the line as well in Los Angeles. As soon as they hopped on, they immediately declared they had no ratings news yet, but based on what they saw on Twitter it felt like the fans had truly responded to the new look and feel of season two. The call was regarding the running time of the episodes. Beginning in 211 the show had to be exactly 42 minutes, not a second over or under. This was the new mandate for all the shows on the network. They also wanted to insert a thirty second intro to the show before the recap to help introduce the concept to new viewers. It would be written and edited by the network, so it wouldn't interrupt our post-production workflow. We understood and supported the idea, although privately we mourned the loss of an additional thirty seconds dedicated to each episode. One of the most painful parts of editing the episodes was cutting scenes that we loved but weren't essential to the story in order to get to time. Luckily Freeform provided a platform for those deleted scenes on social media, but it's never the same as experiencing the scene in the context of the show.

Later that day, as darkness took over and the temperature plummeted, we sought refuge in a local pub. My phone rang again from the same number. This time Matt and Darren were on hold with me. Brian and Kirsten came on and the joy in their voices was immediately apparent. They were thrilled with the ratings. It was on par with the finale of season one. Congratulations were given all the way around. I was over the moon. Another milestone had been achieved. Of course that elation was soon replaced with the anxiety that always plagued me. Would the fans continue to watch once our impact was more apparent? The premiere started shooting on our first day on the job. The story had been written. The tone was set. All we could do was tweak dialogue here and there. Beginning in episode 202, the fans would be exposed to the show according to Todd and Darren. Hopefully they would stay on board. I knew these racing thoughts weren't productive and only cluttered my mind. It was time to get back to work.

# A NEW YEAR

The first day back we gathered everyone in the writer's room to talk about all of our holiday stories and introduce Q. The three-week break seemed to energize all of us, and the premiere's solid ratings put us all in a good mood. Because Monday was our first day back, we were fortunate to be able to watch the show live that evening at five pm with the entire staff over wine and cheese and Twitter. This quickly became a ritual for almost every episode we did on Shadowhunters, a ritual that I never took for granted. It is unbelievably rare for a show to air at a time when the show's writing staff is still together working in one room. The timing was impeccable and provided an opportunity for all of us to enjoy the show together and with the fans.

Our P.A., Jeff Patenaude, a young, talented writer and the sweetest guy you'll ever meet, managed to hook up his computer to a large television monitor that we propped up on chairs in the writer's room so we could watch the show on the Freeform app at 5pm. Jeff executed the plan with a silent, pleasant grace he seemed to do with everything in life. Being a writer's PA is basically like being a waiter on wheels who doubles as an office manager. While I've never done it, I guarantee you I would not only suck at the actual job, but it would be difficult to always maintain a pleasant demeanor while being grossly underpaid and often underappreciated. I always go out of my way to treat the support staff with the utmost respect. We brought over Jeff from our last show GUILT, where he had filled in during the middle of the season when our former assistant encountered immigration issues. Not only was he smart and kind, he was also a decent basketball player. One of the positives of the dilapidated Shadowhunters writer office was an old, rickety basketball hoop set up in the back parking lot. Many days after lunch I would head out with Jeff and whoever else wanted to join to shoot hoops and clear our minds.

Once the television was set up, we poured our wine and watched the show, one eye on the screen, one eye on our twitter feeds. I always struggled with live tweeting because I often find myself lost in the show. While I've already seen multiple versions of the show, I'm always entranced by the way it looks and sounds on air. Because it's compressed over the network broadcast system, it always looks and sounds slightly different than the version I see during the sound mix. I still usually managed to tweet out a few posts, usually compliments. Any attempts to be witty usually failed. I was too distracted. We all shared a great many laughs as the writers read fan comments out loud. It was so rewarding to hear how much the fans loved certain moments we had brought to the show. Shireen, the writer of the episode, looked deeply relieved, knowing how problematic the episode's production had been. None of it was her fault, but nevertheless her name was on the episode and she was happy to see that it turned out okay. I made sure to raise a glass to her that night.

Don't get the wrong idea - the first day back wasn't a non-stop party. We began our discussions about 215, an episode we knew would function a bit like the second half of a two-parter in terms of Sebastian's story with Valentine. The arrival of Aline, Sebastian's cousin, would tighten the vise around our villain and cause him to interrogate his captive in the closet - the real Sebastian Verlac. This would be a huge reveal and answer a lot of the audience's questions as well as ask more. It would also create edge-of-your-seat suspense when the real Sebastian breaks out and tries to stop imposter Sebastian from carrying out his plan. Add the Imposter's murder of the real Sebastian and the reveal that the imposter is actually Valentine's son, Jonathan Morgenstern, and you have yourself an episode full of awesomeness.

It felt like this episode was the opportune time to play the story of Simon getting framed for murder, one of my favorite Simon plot lines from the books. Simon was at his lowest point, more vulnerable than he's ever been after Clary shattered his heart in the previous episode. It would also be an elegant way to bring Luke and Ollie into a head-on collision over Simon and propel Ollie closer to the truth about the shadow world. That procedural element, while seemingly simple, was anything but. The breaking of the story proved to be one of the most difficult ones of the series. Whether it was the addition of a new voice and new rhythm in the room, or the delicacies of delivering a procedural story full of clues, the process wasn't easy. It often felt too burdened by plot. Too much was happening in a single episode. So over time we kept pruning away story to dedicate more screen time to character moments. After we pitched it to the network and they read the initial outline, they felt the same way we did. It still felt like there was too much there, so we continued to prune away and simplify the plot in favor of more character moments.

The character of Heidi turned out to be a happy accident for us and the fandom. I wish I could tell you we knew exactly how she was going to be used in further seasons, but I would be lying. Initially we cast Tessa Mossey for this one episode. We all loved her performance, and the character who had this bizarre obsession with vampires to the point that she spent her weekend nights getting fed on by the bloodsuckers. It was in the early days of the season 3a writer's room when someone came up with the brilliant idea that Raphael dug up Heidi's corpse and turned her into a vampire to see if she was a daylighter. Heidi's character would take the place of the great book villain Maureen Brown (whose name was already used in season one), a vampire obsessed with Simon. When we later told Alberto that we were planning on bringing Tessa back and Heidi would play a large role in Simon's life in season 3a, he broke into a sweet grin, admitting that they had begun seeing each other after her first episode. A relationship born in the shadow world. I was beaming.

Exploring the darker side of Magnus and his tragic personal history had been a priority of ours since we started. Sure, I loved the funny, flamboyant Magnus who made flippant jokes over a martini, but I was more interested in the other side. Someone who had lived that long had not only sampled the finer things in life, but he had also suffered great loss and pain as he paid witness to a parade of loved ones dying one by one. The death of his mother was touched upon in season 2a with his retrieval of the Keris blade from India - the very blade she used to take her own life. After being exposed to the agony rune in 211, I loved the idea that the torture had re-opened the trove of memories that Magnus had been successfully repressing for the past two hundred or so years. We saw flickers of those memories in the flashbacks in 211. We knew we would pay them off later, and 215 offered us the opportunity to not only see the boy discover his mother's body, but also showcase the first time he used his magic to kill another living thing. This memory would haunt him and trigger a bout of depression, which he would keep from Alec, too afraid of how Alec would react if he knew the truth. In the end he would come clean, and their relationship would be stronger for it. There was much discussion about adding plot to the story but in the end, I knew simplicity was our best friend. My favorite Malec stories were pure emotional character arc, no plot added. This was one of them.

In the end, episode 215 aka "Problem of Memory" is one of the strongest of season two. Director Peter Deluise, the son of the famous actor Dom and a good friend of Matt Hastings, delivered one strong scene after the next with a nice visual flair that never got in the way of the storytelling. Kat and Alberto deliver one of their best performances to date. Each of them experiencing heartbreak over their crumbling relationship feels so honest and true. Isaiah was particularly strong as he struggled to accept the reality that this young man he considered a son was a killer thanks to his demon blood. The scene at the Jade Wolf where Luke intimates to Clary the horrible affect demon blood can have on one's behavior gives me chills. Sebastian Verlac hits his stride and Will Tudor is phenomenal throughout. Harry and Matt, as they always do, work so well together. Alec's helpless frustration and Harry's pain go together like chocolate and peanut butter. An episode full of pure, undiluted Malec was the ideal counterbalance to the heavy plot machinations that took place in the other stories.

Admittedly, there is a cringeworthy moment of film in the show that I bemoan to this day. At the very end of the episode we wanted to reveal that Sebastian was in reality Valentine's son, Jonathan, who had been severely burned during his time in Edom. For some reason I can't recall, it was decided it would be best to have another actor beside Will Tudor wear the prosthetic burn suit. We were sent photos of the actor in the near completed burn suit, and while we had our reservations, we signed off when we were assured once the suit was completely done it would look a lot better. At the end of the day, all the blame deserves to be placed squarely at our feet, because the final product in 215, 216 and 217 was definitely not one of our shining moments. Names like "burn boy" and "lasagna boy" became part of our vernacular for a while.

215 was decidedly low on visual effects on purpose, not that the visual effects that are present aren't amazing. A shot I particularly love is when Simon uses the wooden stake to stab Quinn in the heart and he disintegrates to ash right in front of Simon's horrified face. Also the peek into the city of glass, Alicante, toward the end of the show is staggering, complete with demon towers and a flowing waterfall. During a ten-episode season we target which episodes will cost more and then create certain episodes that can be done at a lower budget in order to compensate for the overages. Usually the premiere and finale are more expensive, as well as a mid-season extravaganza. In season 2b both 214 and 216 were pegged to be a visual effects feast.

# CANADA O CANADA

To launch the production of season 2b and attend the table-read, Darren and I met at LAX on a brisk Thursday morning to fly to Toronto. Normally we would fly back after the table read on Friday, but we wanted to be there on the first day of principal photography for season 2b, which was that Monday. Also, Doug McCullough, our production designer, was throwing a huge party that Saturday evening at his home and invited us and a number of folks from the show, including the entire cast. And if we were in town on Sunday, Matt Hastings suggested we conduct our tone meeting for episode 211 over a luxurious brunch at a fancy hotel. Needless to say (more about "needless to say" later), the decision to stay in Toronto over the weekend wasn't a hard one.

When we touched down in Canada, it was abundantly clear that it was now considerably colder than it was during our autumn trek. As a couple of born and bred Southern California boys, we bundled up like we were headed into the arctic. Our driver from production who picked us up was as kind as can be, our chat on the way back to the hotel pleasantly non-political. Once we checked in we immediately hopped on a notes call for the 215 outline with the network and

Allison and the writing staff in L.A. The call wasn't short. They had extensive notes, but good ones as usual. Once the call ended, we hurried downstairs to eat dinner, too tired to brave the cold to search for something outside. Strangely the hotel restaurant was closed. We could either order room service or go out. We ended up going out, a single block, to Wahlburgers, where I had smartly never been before.

The next morning we headed into the studio, where the office staff appeared refreshed after their nice six-week break. Matt and Doug gave us a quick tour of the new sets, many which were still being constructed. Production hadn't started yet, so the sound stages were lit up by house lights, the sound of hammers and saws echoing throughout the cavernous space. Outside of the wardrobe department, we spotted Will Tudor waiting patiently for his fitting. We had only met over the phone, when we discussed at great lengths our ideas about his character. It was great to finally meet him in the flesh. He was just as charismatic as he was in his audition tape.

We sat down with each of the actors in our makeshift office to fill them in on their upcoming arcs for the next ten episodes and hear any thoughts or questions they might have. The meetings were scheduled every thirty minutes so that we would be available for the production meeting and table read later that afternoon. Now that they had seen our work in the first few episodes of season two, the cast appeared more relaxed and trusting. Kat arrived straight from her training session in the gym. As a book fan, her eyes lit up when we told her our plans for Clary during season 2b. When we explained that we were going to actually dunk her in a water tank that would resemble her landing in Lake Lyn, Kat could barely contain herself. This was an actress who was up for anything that would support the storytelling, even if it meant spending the day underwater in her full wardrobe, boots included. Our take on the discovery of the Mortal Mirror was quite different than the books, and she bought into it wholeheartedly. Kat loved the fact that she would defeat Valentine with her bare hands instead of Raziel killing him like he did in the books. Regarding her schedule, Kat is an actress who loves to work as much as possible, and looking at the schedule for

211, she noticed that she was working less days than usual. Was this the new normal? We assured her that she would work plenty. Clary was and will always be at the center of the show, but we also wanted to spend the screen time exploring these seven other characters. She totally understood.

Dom was next. He was very complimentary about the episodes he had seen, especially the action sequences. Like all the actors, he took his stunt work very seriously, eager to do his own stunts whenever he could. Trained as a dancer, he enjoyed the physical work and looked forward to more of it. He was excited about playing the guilt that would haunt Jace after his accidental slaughter of the downworlders. Being friends with Will Tudor, he was thrilled that they were going to have a heated rivalry onscreen that would end up in a fierce battle to the death. We filled him on his upcoming Herondale name change, his journey to Idris, and his eventual death at the hands of Valentine and his resurrection thanks to Clary and the Angel Raziel. A musician himself, Dom was psyched when we mentioned he would be playing piano. He was also relieved to know more parabatai moments lie ahead. From our first conversation we knew the parabatai relationship was important to him, and he was thrilled that 211 was full of these moments.

Emeraude followed, elegant as always. She was happy to play such a big role in 211 but worried about playing the effects of the yin fen withdrawal. She had no history with drugs whatsoever and was weary that it would come off as fake. We assured her under the directorial guidance of Matt Hastings, she would be excellent. And we weren't wrong. Her performance in 211 was incredible. We filled her in on our idea of exploring her road to recovery while gaining her strength back. Izzy would gradually open up to the others about her addiction, including her mother, and realize that her secrecy would only hinder her recovery. She loved the idea that after being suckered by Sebastian in 211, Izzy would play a huge role in taking him down at the end of the season. When we mentioned that her little brother Max would return to the Institute and she would be in charge of his training, she smiled broadly. This was going to be fun.

Isaiah breezed in, happy as ever. He had proposed to his girlfriend over the holidays and had the glow of the newly engaged. Isaiah loved the idea of Luke having a new partner who was poking into the shadow world, and the fact that he'd continually have to run interference. It would be humorous at times, which would utilize Isaiah's natural comic timing. It would also give Luke more screen-time, which we had been wanting to do from the beginning. It was difficult because Luke didn't live or work at the Institute with the others. His scenes were primarily with Clary, Simon and Maia, and we yearned to broaden his interactions with the rest of the cast. Isaiah was the consummate professional and team player, his experience as an athlete in the NFL teaching him the importance that no one individual was bigger than the show. He understood his role and never once complained. As the elder member of the cast, Isaiah and I had much in common, including teenage daughters the exact same age. After comparing our joyous and frustrating stories, we were comforted by the fact that we weren't alone in our struggles parenting teens.

With six episodes under her belt now, Alisha was more confident and assured than ever. We told her about her burgeoning romantic relationship with Simon and promised it would feel earned and not rushed. While Simon dated Maia and Isabelle at the same time in the books, we wouldn't do that in the show, but we would explore Isabelle's protective instincts when it came to Simon. We talked about exploring Maia's past this season, including how she turned into a werewolf at the hands of her ex-boyfriend Jordan. It was a controversial storyline in the books, and we wanted to treat it as carefully as possible. It would also help set up the character of Jordan Kyle, who we were planning to bring on the show in season 3 if we were lucky enough to get renewed. Alisha was excited and eager to peel the layers of the onion and let the audience learn more about Maia, as were we.

Matt Daddario was night and day from the first time we met him in August. He could not have been more warm and welcoming. Matt was thrilled when we told him that Alec was going to be the Head of the Institute and, like any leader, forced to make difficult moral and ethical decisions. He loved his scenes with Magnus, but he understandably wanted his character to be involved in more than just a love story, no matter how special that love story was. When we told him Alec and Magnus were going to face a rough patch and break up for a few episodes, he was on board but warned us that the fans might riot. We shared a laugh, knowing how much Malec meant to so many fans around the world, but without conflict and growth, they would find the relationship quickly becoming stale.

Harry strolled through the door in his jeans, T-shirt and Counting Crows baseball cap. He was nothing like Magnus Bane, which was a real testament to his tremendous acting ability. He and his wife had just returned from Iceland, and he showed us a few pics from his trip before we delved into Magnus Bane's season 2b journey. Harry was a true artist, always eager to dig deeper. The idea of exploring Magnus' dark side was one he immediately embraced. Like most great actors I've worked, Harry loved being able to play the many sides to his character. We told him that we wanted to use his dancing skills at some point soon but would find just the right place for it so it wouldn't feel forced. When we mentioned the impending break-up with Alec, he smiled knowingly and wished us good luck.

Alberto was up next, our last cast meeting for the day. His positive energy was always infectious, and today was no exception. Alberto felt like he took nothing for granted. He was completely unjaded in the best of ways, in awe of the film-making process and the parade of creative people around him that made it happen. He took the work extremely seriously and it was a pleasure to talk all things Simon with him. As a daylighter, Simon's world would immediately widen, giving him the opportunity to act with more cast members. It would also bring the unwanted attention from Raphael and the other vampires who dream of being able to step out of the shadows. I loved the idea that even though Simon could now be outside and part of the real world, he could never be normal. He would always be a vampire. And this realization would be heartbreaking, for Simon and the audience. No matter how much he tried, he could never go back to the way things used to be. Simon's original music would finally come to fruition, which for a kid who's done a lot of musical theater in his time, was extremely exciting for Alberto. Having read all the books, he was thrilled we were tackling the Simon framed for murder plotline, and relieved Simon wouldn't be dating two girls at the same time.

After a quick lunch, we headed into the conference room with Matt Hastings, Chris "line producer extraordinaire" Hatcher, Doug the production designer and our wonderful costume designer Shelley Mansell to give them all a brief season 2b pitch. This would allow them to be ahead of the big set builds and location moves that we were planning and could then budget their money and time accordingly. They were great listeners, on the edge of their seats as I took them through the Seelie Forest to the yin fen drug den and the journey to Lake Lynn, climaxing in a feast of visual effects thanks to our friend Angel Raziel. Soon their fellow department heads began to trickle in as the 211 production meeting was about to begin. All the heads of the departments that we hear on the speaker phone every episode were there in person, and it was so rewarding to hear their warm reaction to the first three finished episodes they'd seen on Netflix with the rest of the world. Led by the first assistant director Siluck Saysanasy, we went scene-by-scene through the script with Matt asking various questions to make sure he had what he needed "on the day" (meaning when he's shooting that scene).

The table read was next. Kirsten Creamer, who normally listened in with her colleagues at the network in L.A., was there in person. She had flown up for the occasion, and it was great to see her. She had begun her career at the network as an intern and quickly rose through the ranks to become an executive on several of their shows. Kirsten was not only wickedly smart, but she was always so kind and supportive. The table read went well, with Matt reading the scene description to keep the energy up. A flat reading of scene description during a table-read is a major buzzkill and can often garner unnecessary notes. Thankfully Matt's theatrical reads kept things moving and entertaining (he was an actor in his younger years). Afterwards we hopped on the phone with the writing staff in L.A. to hear their thoughts while Kirsten spoke with her colleagues back in Los Angeles. Kirsten then sat down with us and gave us the network's notes while the staff emailed their thoughts for us to incorporate during our pass on the script that we'd work on over the weekend.

That night Kirsten treated me, Darren, Matt Hastings, and Margo

Klewans to a wonderful meal at our favorite steakhouse in Toronto, Harbour Sixty. Many laughs, much wine and a lot of food was shared, and a great time was had by all. Oddly, when I awoke the next morning, I was not only greeted by a mild hangover but my big toe on my left foot was on fire with searing pain. Did I sleep on it weird? How do you even sleep on a big toe? When I met Darren down in the lobby to head out to a breakfast place across the street and mentioned my strange, new malady, he immediately said the word "gout." Little known secret about Darren - the man is a walking encyclopedia of vast medical knowledge. I had learned over the years that his diagnoses were rarely wrong. But gout? Isn't that what medieval kings suffered from drinking too much wine and eating ridiculously rich foods? And then I remembered the fried calamari and lamb chops at dinner the night before, not to mention the river of wine that I drank. In general my eating and drinking habits hadn't exactly been stellar as of late. The pressure of running a show certainly didn't help. Now it seemed my body was telling me to chill. Doctor Darren gave me my prescription - no fried foods, no sugar, no alcohol. Over time the pain would go away.

I took my new diet seriously, but of course the timing couldn't have been worse. That evening we had dinner with Marc Kahn, who was up in Toronto to meet the crew, especially our sound and coloring teams who he worked with remotely on every episode. I dutifully drank my water and ate my fish. Afterwards we hopped into an Uber and went to Doug McCullough's big winter party. His beautiful house was packed to the gills, tipsy guests laughing and having the time of their lives. I don't remember the last time I was at a party totally sober, but it had been awhile. I managed to have a nice chat with Joe Lasarov, the director of episode 204 who was now working on DESIGNATED SURVIVOR. Outside an Uber minivan pulled up and pretty much the entire Shadowhunters cast spilled out and into the party, their combined charisma lighting up the house like fireworks. They had just come from dinner together, and their easy camaraderie with each other was on full display. The cast was a tight bunch who spent a lot of time together. Filming a show on location tends to either bond actors together or split them apart, and this cast was clearly bonded. The idea of a found family in the show had crossed over to real life. As a showrunner, it was a wonderful thing to witness.

The next morning we met Matt Hastings for our 211 tone meeting over brunch at the Ritz Carlton Hotel. It was a mere four blocks from our hotel but in the fierce winter chill, it felt like a mile. The brunch buffet was loaded with every rich food imaginable and a dessert table that looked like something out of Charlie and the Factory. While Matt sipped champagne and piled his tray high, I sipped my water and ate egg whites. We went over every scene like we always do with the directors, but because Matt knew the show and actors so well, our tone meetings were always brief. He was a big fan of the script and had only one real note about the summoning of Azazel at the Institute. Originally Clary was already present when the greater demon appeared, but Matt wanted her to arrive in dramatic fashion. We didn't understand the logic, but Matt had clearly had a strong vision of the way the sequence would play out, and we trusted him completely. His visual taste for the show had proven to be impeccable. We returned to the hotel and implemented the various notes from the writers, the network and Matt into the shooting script. We then sent it down to Joey in L.A. to proof and distribute to the cast and crew. Another script was locked and loaded, ready to go to camera tomorrow.

That evening we had dinner with Harry Shum at one of his favorite sushi places in Toronto, JaBistro. Harry had reached out to us in L.A. a few weeks earlier and invited us to dinner but had to cancel due to a cold. Darren and I braved the chill and walked a half mile onto a dark street, where we stepped down a flight of stairs into this cool, minimalist Japanese restaurant. Harry was there to greet us, and we had a wonderful meal, the conversation warm and carefree. Harry was always eager to use his physical prowess for his character and was thrilled when we told him how cool his battle with Iris Rouse turned out in 208. We told him there would be more of that ahead. When the bill came we offered to pay but Harry insisted it was his treat. I left thinking how blessed I was to be working with such a talented, warm-hearted human being.

I woke up Monday morning and my toe was noticeably better. Darren's prescribed diet had worked wonders. Our flight was at noon, leaving us enough time to spend some time on set with the shooting crew. These were the people who were on the front lines of the filmmaking, on set working fourteen or fifteen hour days five days a week. The camera operators, grips, hair and make-up personnel, script supervisor, props and set decorators. The assistant directors and cinematographers were on set every other episode, but these people were there for every single scene. Not until I first directed back on Smallville did I have a full appreciation of how important it was to have a happy crew. The scene that was being shot that morning involved Luke and Ollie talking in Luke's SUV parked in one of our dark alleys only to be interrupted by Maia. We had never met Alexandra Ordolis, the actress who played Ollie. She was charming and seemingly not nervous at all shooting her first scene on the show. We spoke with her, Isaiah and Alisha, and chatted with as many crew members as we could before we had to leave for the airport. As we hugged Matt goodbye and walked back through the studio, I sensed the show was in a good place. This ten-episode season would be even stronger than the last.

# THE ATL

We returned to L.A. knowing we'd be hitting the road again the following week, this time to Atlanta, Georgia for the Atlanta TV Fest hosted by TV/Film school of Savannah College of Art and Design (SCAD). They had reached out and invited us back in November, but with everything going on I pretty much forgot about it. The writer's room had been busy working on 216 and pitched us what they had so far, Pete Binswanger taking us through the story. This episode would hit many touchstones from the books, including Clary and Jace's journey to Idris and their little underwater adventure in Lake Lyn. The fans were surely going to flip. The Simon and Maia Yom Kippur story blew me away. I was deeply moved by Simon's guilt from the previous episode and his need for atonement. As a non-religious but cultural Jew, I was excited by the prospect of using Judaic traditions to help shape Simon's character. In 205, when Michael Reisz suggested that Simon recite the mourner's kaddish for the recently deceased Jocelyn, I got goosebumps. It was such a beautiful expression of Simon's love for his friend. A Yom Kippur dinner with his family where he would feel compelled to tell them about his vampiric behavior was even better. Add Maia by his side, where we could learn more about her backstory and her own guilt regarding her family, and I was totally on board. I was admittedly concerned about introducing Grandma Bubbie in the flesh. We worried it could feel too broad, too "sitcom-ish", but Pete and the writers persuaded us it would work.

We had wanted to bring Robert Lightwood back into the show for a while, and 216 aka "Day of Atonement" was the right story for him to be involved in. As an envoy from the Clave, he would be the one to tell Alec that the Clave in fact was not in possession of the soul sword and had been lying about it all this time. Alec would then have to wrestle with the decision whether to tell Magnus or keep it a secret. With these three stories, there was little room for anything else in the episode. We had learned by now that three stories was the maximum we could execute in our allotted 42 minutes without the show feeling too rushed. But we knew an episode without any sign of Magnus and Luke would be problematic. Yes, their absence could be explained by their off-screen journey to see the Seelie Queen, but we knew the fans would be upset. I was upset. We ended up crafting a scene between Magnus and Luke at Magnus' apartment after they had returned, where they discussed whether to believe the Queen's conspiracy theories about the Shadowhunters. At this point in the show, thanks to Robert's confession, the audience knew she was actually telling the truth. But Magnus had complete faith in Alec that if anything like that was even remotely true, he would come forward and tell him. Of course, this was all building to their fated breakup in 217. Pete wrote the scene. We shot the scene. But in the end there was no time for it in the cut and we made the painful decision to cut it. These choices always killed me.

When it aired, the bit of backlash came as expected, but I was enormously proud of the episode. Pete delivered a really strong script right out of the gate. Often times that first writer's draft goes through many different permutations before it becomes a shooting script, but much of that first draft is in the show. Paul Wesley did a fantastic job directing, able to deliver brilliant cinematic scope as well as capturing terrific performances from the cast. The shoot was far from easy. All the Idris scenes were shot at a remote location in the woods in freezing temperatures. It was far enough from the studio that some cast and crew stayed at a local hotel to reduce the driving time there and back. Paul was not only fighting the elements but also a flu, which he refused to let take him down. The actors were all really impressed with his directing and went out of their way to tell us how much they enjoyed the experience. Paul had been on a hit show for eight seasons. He knew exactly what they were going through and could relate to them like no one else. Later when we mixed the show months later, we invited Paul, who we had never met in person. He couldn't have been nicer and offered up some good notes. We told him if he was ever into directing another episode, we'd love to have him back. And we'd make sure it wasn't in the dead of winter in the middle of the woods.

Atlanta would be quick jaunt. We would fly out on a Friday morning and I would return early Sunday morning, in time to watch the Super Bowl with my family. Saturday was our big day at the festival. We would first do a few interviews, there would be a screening of episode 206, due to air in two days, and then we'd do a panel with Kat and Alisha. They put us up at the swanky Four Seasons, which was generous and luxurious. As soon as we checked in we jumped on a notes call with the network about the 215 script, and then ate dinner at the hotel. With no sign of gout in a good while, I ordered the lamb chops.

Saturday morning, we met Kat and Alisha at the hotel getting their hair and make-up done. Alisha had come in on the red eye from L.A. but you'd never know it. Kat had come in the night before from Toronto, and they both looked radiant. The ever bubbly Catherine Graves from the network's publicity team met us and guided us into a van that drove us to a venue near campus. Before the panel we did a series of interviews, but not with the press - they were students from the school. The questions were more about breaking into the business of writing for television rather than that actual show, and their innocent, wide-eyed aura was refreshing. Afterward we met the moderator for our panel, Damian Holbrook, a journalist and Shadowhunters fan from TV Guide who had been flown in from Philadelphia for the occasion. After a few photos, we were led into the dark theater, where the audience was watching the end of 206 on the big screen. It was a special experience to be able to watch the show with hundreds of people, even if it was just a few minutes. The Iron Sisters' Citadel never looked more grand.

Once the episode ended, we all took to the stage and Damian asked us each questions followed by questions from the audience. It went by far too quickly, as all these things do. One minute I'm walking onto the stage and then boom, it's done and I'm left to ponder how incomprehensible and lame I probably sounded. As we walked off the stage, fans surrounded Kat and Alisha as they always do. One student introduced themselves to me as a writer who wanted to write and produce television in the vein of Shadowhunters. They were clearly bright and over time we exchanged a few nice words over Twitter. That night Darren and I went out to dinner with Kat and Alisha to a restaurant Kat had heard about. In the lobby on the way out, we ran into an old colleague of ours, Michael Roberts, a senior executive at the CW who we first met in our screenwriting career and then reunited with during our first year on SMALLVILLE when he was an executive at the WB. Michael was ironically in Atlanta for THE VAMPIRE DIARIES 200th episode party and was about to see Paul Wesley. We told him to give Paul our best and headed out.

Dinner with Kat and Alisha was delightful and delicious. It was great to spend time with them away from set where we could all relax and get to know each other. They are both smart, driven actors with high IQs. Throughout my tenure on the show, I continually had to remind myself how young Kat was, considering her high level of maturity, grace and intellect. Over dessert, I couldn't help but fill them in on a few spoilers that were coming down the pipeline for each of their characters. As we all said our goodbyes and goodnights in the lobby of the Four Seasons, I again realized how blessed I was to be part of something that would enable us to be here in the lap of luxury to talk about this show that had grown so close to my heart.

# SUBMERGED

The mystery of the ocean and the wonder of being underwater is something I've always been obsessed with. Growing up in Los Angeles, I spent countless hours in the dark waters. Too cowardly to scuba-dive, I've always loved watching films that took place underwater. JAWS, THE DEEP, TITANIC, THE ABYSS, even 47 METERS DOWN are my jam. When I read the story of Clary landing underwater in Lake Lyn and accidentally swallowing the lake water, I knew it would be awesome to film her in a tank. I also knew on this show's budget we couldn't afford to travel to a water tank, essentially a location day, to film a quarter of a script page - roughly fifteen seconds of screen time. It would only be worthwhile to produce if we shot more pages of the show there. So we concocted this idea that Clary's underwater experience in the lake would stay with her as recurring dreams and hallucinations through several episodes, dreams that would eventually clue her into the realization that the mortal mirror is actually Lake Lyn. That's why the objects underwater appeared as dual reflections. It was cool and clever, and an example of how sometimes, when faced with a budget issue, it can lead you to an idea that was more exciting than what you previously imagined.

The sequences that first appeared in 216 and continued through 217 and 218 were shot in a swimming pool at a rec center nearby with a scuba-diving camera operator and an underwater camera, as well as our regular crew. That day it was just Kat and Dom and heated blue pool water. Months later, with the addition of the strands of swaying seaweed, the schools of darting fish, and the fast-approaching dual swords provided by the masterminds at Folks VFX, it would become Lake Lyn underwater.

217 aka "A Dark Reflection" was the only Shadowhunters episode we pitched to the network where they "blew it up," meaning they told us to go back to the drawing board. The original idea involved going into Jace's unconscious mind and sorting through his various memories to try to save him. Of course, we do a similar story the following season in 308, but at this time they felt it was too similar to an episode they were doing on STITCHERS, a show on the network that aired the same night. To the writer's room's credit, they quickly rallied and came up with the idea you see in the episode today. Sebastian and Valentine, father and son, uneasily reunited as they try to hunt down the mortal mirror, committing murder and mayhem every step of the way. It would provide an opportunity to bring back our favorite Iron Sister Cleophus, now in captivity at the hands of Valentine. While the auto body location set was not among my favorites, it was interesting to see her out of her element and paying penance for the terrible things she had done in her past.

I loved the idea of Isabelle being responsible for training Max and struggling with the fact that she was about to put her baby brother in harm's way. And the tragic irony of Isabelle teaching him how to use his tracking skills, the very skills that would lead to his brutal assault, was icing on the cake. The scene on the rooftop with the pigeons is one of my favorite visual effect shots of the entire series. We knew any opportunity to have Izzy spend time with Simon was golden, not just because their chemistry was off the charts, but because they were canon in the books. The book fandom knew they would end up as a couple eventually, so any time we could get them together and hint at their future was special. Alberto and Emeraude were also two Latinx actors who had an enormous fan base in Brazil and throughout Latin America that worshipped them. We also imagined Simon being great with a younger brother/nephew type, and knew those scenes with Max would feel genuine and make you love Simon even more than you already did.

Izzy and Maia's tense cross in the Jade Wolf would be our short but poignant homage to their story in the books. Alisha and Emeraude played well off of each other with just enough sass without turning it into the Real Girlfriends of the Shadow World. The notion that Isabelle recognized a broken heart in Maia's past displayed Izzy's keen intuitive abilities. The hint of Jordan in Maia's backstory permeates the entire episode, setting up his reveal in 218. Maia's scene at the end of the episode with Simon is bursting with the magical chemistry that imbues the show with a real sense of love and respect between two people who are told they shouldn't be together but are drawn to each other nevertheless. I began shipping them way back in 203. 216 made me ship them even harder. And now at the end of this scene, I was ready to see them together.

The Malec subplot and dreaded break-up was also there from the beginning. Magnus would have scenes with Luke to talk about his mind space, which was a nice rapport we didn't often see on the show. The makeshift Cape Cod dinner over candlelight would be an elegant prelude to what would become an uncomfortable scene for many to watch. Hollie Overton's script was masterfully directed by Jeff Hunt, a seasoned director we had never worked with before. His visual style was so strong and assured. The performances were all spot on. The only scene that made me cringe - you guessed it - is Burn Boy and his fight in the park with Jace. We tried to cut away from the burn suit as much as possible but at the end of the day, it is what it is. I did love Dot saving the day by creating a portal to help Jace and Clary escape. Sacrifice is a leading theme that runs throughout the books and the show, and anytime a character could behave in that heroic kind of way, I embraced it. As Jocelyn's best friend, Dot would do anything to protect her late friend's daughter, and she does in what would come to be her final act on the show. Vanessa Matsui did a wonderful job playing both her strength and vulnerability, and we only wish we could have had the time to use her more.

From the beginning of breaking the episode, we knew we wanted to end with Max in jeopardy at the hands of Sebastian. This would be one of the better cliffhangers we've ever done on the show. In the books Sebastian killed Max, so books fans would be gasping, wondering if we were going to follow that path. We had already proven that we were willing to go outside of book canon in a major way, as evidenced by Jocelyn's shocking death. You'd have no choice but to watch that next episode to find out how things turned out for the poor child.

Post-production on 2b was now in full swing. Our days were spent in editing bays, mixing stages, coloring rooms, the writer's room, and of course our office - writing, talking, pitching, listening to Bon Iver, Haim and our homegrown Shadowhunters playlist, titled "Between the Wars," which was growing every day. The days were long but thrilling, full of unexpected moments of inspiration and joy. Monday at 5pm continued to be a wine and cheese viewing party throughout the run of 2a. The ratings had fallen back to earth and were now up and down, their trajectory something I had been understandably obsessed with. Every time the ratings dropped I took it personally, feeling that I had failed the network - the very people who had trusted us to make it better. Young Pete Binswanger, a true millennial with a big fat heart, tried to make me feel better by explaining that no one he knew watched broadcast television live anymore. They either watched the show on the app or Hulu. But I still felt bad, and couldn't help but express my guilt to our executives Brian and Kirsten at the network. They were nothing but supportive and assured me that they all were really happy with the creative direction of the show and not to worry about those overnight numbers. Of course, that didn't stop me from going online every Tuesday afternoon around 2pm to see the numbers come in.

The news of a GLAAD nomination was a nice acknowledgement for the show. Shadowhunters had already won a Teen Choice Award for Matt Daddario, which was exciting but not quite as prestigious or meaningful as a GLAAD nomination. We were in fine company, right alongside such classic shows as SHAMELESS and ORPHAN BLACK. It was especially heartening for Michael

Reisz who ran point on crafting this special relationship during season one, penning the fan favorite and my favorite episode of the first season, 112 aka "Malec." I was thrilled for Michael, and Harry and Matt. Darren and I were offered a chance to go to the awards ceremony, but we felt that this was Michael's night. He should be the one to bask in the glory of the work that was done in season one. It was the celebration of a love story between two individuals who, despite their glaring cultural and age differences, shared a love that was more powerful than any obstacle that could get in their way. Love wins. When the show won the award I could barely believe it. Harry and Matt were flown out to L.A. from Toronto for the ceremony and gracefully accepted the award among a cheering ballroom. I was beaming with pride.

I have been blessed to have been involved in hundreds of episodes of television, many of which I am incredibly proud of. Episode 218 aka "Awake, Arise and Be Fallen" ranks at, or very near, the top of that list. The story and script, the directing and acting, the editing, the production design, the cinematography, the props - every single department achieved absolute greatness. As we all sat in the writer's room staring at a blank white board, I had no idea at the time that it was going to be that good. But the bones of the show were promising from the get-go. A child's life would be hanging in the balance for the duration of the episode, so the dramatic stakes would be sky high. In the book Max's death was a bold, shocking plot move that worked really well. But in the show we felt the child's death would simply be too much of a downer that would darken the already dark last act of season 2b in a way that was too grim even for us. But he could certainly be severely injured, and we could spend an episode wondering whether he'll live or die. The all-knowing legion of book fans would think they knew what was going to happen only to be thrown at the end.

The suspense would be ratcheted up even more with Sebastian lurking near the child's hospital bed, waiting for his chance to be alone with him so he can finish what he started and prevent him from revealing his true identity. This dramatic spine would keep the audience on the edge of their seats throughout the show and would provide a glimpse of Sebastian at his most desperate low point.

It would also bring back Robert and Maryse Lightwood to the Institute and create a rare Lightwood family reunion. Even in the most dire of circumstances, it was nice to see the whole family in one room.

Maia, Simon and Luke dealing with a newly turned werewolf was a fascinating story that would have book fans jumping up and down at the introduction of Bat Velasquez, another beloved character from the books. We knew Simon witnessing a werewolf's first turn and trying to assist Maia could be rife with comic potential, but casting Kevin Alves as Bat brought a sense of humor to the proceedings that was entirely unexpected and terrific fun. Kevin was a great local actor (and competitive ice skater) who we knew would recur throughout the series. Acting as Bat's caretakers would bring Maia and Simon closer together and provide an opportunity for Simon and the audience to hear Maia talk about her tragic past with Jordan. Alisha's performance sends chills up my spine every time I watch it.

Luke would finally get a proper story of his own, forced to right the wrongs of his pack and become the new alpha. Isaiah is always good, but he is particularly strong throughout the episode. He plays off everyone in this episode so well, comedically with Ollie and her girlfriend Sam, a father figure with Maia and Simon, and a moral Alpha with his New York pack. Ollie and her girlfriend would fold into that story at the Jade Wolf, planting a tiny surveillance camera that would pay off at the end and bring Ollie closer to discovering the truth about the Shadow World.

On the verge of their breakup, Magnus would reflect on his relationship with Alec through a series of flashbacks. This would be our redemption for the mistake we made in 207. We could now explore their "first time" together in a deeper, more meaningful way that would shed light on that special night. The darkening of each rose petal to signal that time was running out was a nice poetic touch that would hasten Magnus' painful decision to end his relationship with Alec. He simply loved Alec too much, and that love was clouding his judgement as the High Warlock of Brooklyn, putting the entire downworld population at risk.

There was a lot going on in the episode, but due to the elegant

134

construction of the story and Jamie Gorenberg's fine script, none if it felt cluttered or rushed. The story lines all felt totally organic and distinct yet seemed to somehow emotionally support each other. Based on what was on the page, I knew it was going to be good. But I had no idea how much of an impact this first-time episodic director would have on the material, lending it an artistry I could only have dreamed of.

It turned out Amanda Michael Row was a masterful director disguised as a frustrated assistant. By the time the show had begun prep I knew what great taste she had based on the number of cool demon designs she had found and successfully pitched that ended up on the show. But I had no idea how good of a director she was. When every single department delivers flawless work in a single episode, one has to tip their hand to the person at the helm. Amanda's directing was jaw-dropping. Her shot-making was interesting and dynamic and always in support of telling the story. The two action sequences in the episode were some of the best in the entire series. Luke fighting Russell and Sebastian taking down the guards in the subcells totally blew my mind. The editing was spectacular here and in every scene. And the performances... my God. Every actor was at their best. It is probably the only episode in the series where not a single moment made me cringe. I felt privileged to have been a part of something so well done, and the fact that it was the very first episode of a director who was about to embark on a monstrous career made it that much more special.

The last two episodes of the season would be helmed by a single director who would block shoot the two scripts as if it were a movie. This was possible because we were far enough ahead in the writer's room that we were able to complete the last two finished scripts by the time 219 was scheduled to go in front of the camera. Block shooting would allow us to deliver bigger production value for both episodes and have them directed by our own Matt Hastings. The network had some bad experiences in the past with block shooting and was skeptical at first, but Darren and I assured them it would work out fine. We had block shot the last three series we did and never had problems. They agreed to give it a try, comfortable that Matt was directing them.

Bryan Q. Miller would write 219 and Darren and I would write 220. Once the shows were broken in the room and pitched together to the network, the writers were officially done. I couldn't believe we were so close to the end of our time together. It felt like we arrived in the writer's room yesterday and now we'd all be here only two more weeks to help create the last stories most of us would work on together. By this time we realized that many of the writers were ready to move on to other things. Whether they were sick and tired of us or wanted to flex their creative muscles on a different show, we'll never know, but it was clear that this current line-up of brilliant, funny, big-hearted writers was going away soon.

The two episodes didn't take long to come together. Many of the tent pole moments were already established from the books. I was excited about introducing another pivotal character from the books, Magnus' good friend and fellow warlock Catarina Loss. As a nurse in the mundane world, we saw great potential with her character throughout the series and were thrilled when we cast the actress Sophia Walker to play her. I had an epiphany that Catarina should adopt Madzie and raise her like her own. I imagined Catarina enrolling her in school and teaching her how to use her powers for good. It was a spin-off I'd watch in a heartbeat. The writers were on a roll and eager to get to the end. They were firing on all cylinders and the pitch for the last two episodes, led by Q and Michael Reisz, was awesome. When I heard Q describe a bloodied, near-dead Sebastian crawling out of the ocean and onto the beach, using his own blood to draw a hexagram that would release the legion of flying demons that would eventually become what he utters in his dying breath - "mother...", I knew it was going to be special.

Q is an exceptionally gifted writer with the ability to pen hysterically wry dialogue, especially evidenced in the quips spoken during his elaborately choreographed action sequences. His script for 219 aka "Hail and Farewell" was buoyant and humorous in a way the show hadn't been up to that point. It was also tender and poignant, with many great moments for the actors. Kat shines in these last two episodes, the growth and maturity of Clary clearly evident. Her "love scene" with Jace out on the Institute rooftop when she's drawing runes on his bare chest to try and track down Jonathan is so utterly absurd but also so damn romantic and sensual - an example of a scene you could only really see on Shadowhuunters. Their scene at the end is one of my favorite Kat performances, when she utters Q's memorable line "I'm tired of being afraid."

The action scenes on the page were spectacular. Many viewers don't realize that action sequences often come from the mind of a writer and not a director and can be specifically mapped out in the script. That's not what it's always like. Sometimes the director has a vision for a stunt sequence and simply dictates it to the writer. Q is a force of nature with his action. His descriptive words fly off the page, and much of what you see in the show began in his head. Matt Hastings, who is a master of action as a director, takes those words and makes it his own with the help of the extraordinary stunt coordinator Darren McGuire. The Forsaken attack was slated to be staged in many different locations, including a naval museum on the deck of a ship, before Matt and his team settled on a mausoleum at a cemetery. The gothic location fit well, and the use of funeral-goers that have now been turned into demon-possessed murderers was a cool, ironic touch. The face-off between Jace, Sebastian and Isabelle on the bridge is one of the best action scenes in the series. Isabelle cracking her whip as she stalks toward Sebastian, reading him the riot act, is Emeraude at her finest. Sebastian telling Jace "I don't need your pity. I need your life" is the quintessential Q action quip.

Because the Seelie Queen's relationship with Simon would turn flirtatious in 219, we decided it would be best and much less creepy if she made herself appear closer to his age in this episode. As we were about to begin auditions, Matt Hastings received a text from Sarah Hyland with a photo of Sarah dressed up as a Seelie with the mysterious words "Seelie Queen?" Sarah had by now become part of the cast family, spending time up in Toronto with Dom whenever she could. He sent us the photo and we thought she looked great. But was she serious? She was already busy shooting "Modern Family" and it seemed like such a small role for someone of her stature. But it turned out she was indeed serious. We were thrilled that she was interested but were concerned how we could continue to utilize her throughout the series due to her Modern Family schedule. The network explained her involvement would be "a huge get" for the show, and since the Seelie Queen could adjust her age and appearance at her whim, if Sarah wasn't available in the future we could simply cast another actress to play the older Queen. After clearing her appearance with Modern Family and ABC, Sarah flew up to Toronto for a few days to shoot her part in both 219 and 220. She wasn't feeling a hundred percent during the shoot, but she was fantastic - a total pro who delivered everything we asked of her and more.

Episode 220 aka "Beside Still Water" was a joy to write. The writer's room had crafted a strong episode and outline, and Darren and I dove headfirst into the script without the distraction of having to think about the next episode. The quietude also helped. The writers had all left the building, so the offices were as quiet as still water. As was our norm, Darren and I split up the script to pen the first draft. We then exchanged our work and tweaked each other's pages before getting together and going through the whole draft together. The process usually took a week tops, and this script was no different.

Instead of Valentine dying at the hands of Angel Raziel like he did in the books, we thought it would be more emotionally satisfying for Clary to kill her own father, her venom and hatred even more heightened after Valentine killed Jace. Matt directed the hell out of this action sequence, and Kat and Alan Van Sprang each delivered an epic performance. Jace's dying moments on the shore of Lake Lyn, intercut with Alec feeling his pain back at the Institute and Kat's emotional reaction, is one of my favorite sequences in the series. Alec buckling to his knees in the Institute and Matt Daddario's anguished performance breaks my heart every time I've seen it, as does Kat's silent wail and the tears that stream down her angelic face. To voice the all-powerful Angel Raziel, we reached out to our old colleague Anthony Head, who we met on DOMINION and cast in GUILT. He lent his usual gravitas to the role and made Raziel sound even more ominous and formidable than we could have imagined.

Because we had budgeted wisely and produced several episodes under our normal pattern, the finale had the resources necessary to deliver massive cinematic scope that had never been done on the show. The use of a drone camera during many of the sequences certainly helped, as well as the extraordinary locations. Thanks to the legend John Rakich and his top-notch locations department, we were able to secure an intersection and several streets in the heart of downtown Toronto on a weekend afternoon for the wraith attack. Matt Hastings, the actors and Folks VFX delivered a sequence that is mind blowing in scope and cinematic wonder. Then there's Alec, Magnus and Izzy on the beach trying to seal the demonic rift while fending off a flying, fireball-vomiting wraith demon. Alec running along the sand dodging explosions shouting "Magnus!" over and over is thrilling. And all the work in the woods, hours away from our studio, with Jace and Clary battling Malachi's execution squad, then Valentine, and then of course the reckoning with Raziel, took it to another level. Much careful, creative planning went into it, where parts of Valentine and Clary talking to Raziel were actually shot on a green screen stage at our studio. When edited together and with the skies colored to match, it is seamless upon the final viewing. Jace and Clary tied up in Malachi's tent was also shot at the studio in order to better maximize our days on location.

The last act of the finale was built on moments that would propel the viewer into feeling like they absolutely had to watch another season to see how it would all play out. But before those moments, we wanted to have a party at the Hunter's Moon to celebrate the victory and have all the characters together under one roof, smiling and hugging and sharing the love. It would let the viewer exhale and enjoy for a few minutes before shit was about to get real. We were finally able to use a song of Kat's that she gave us early on when we were beginning to design Simon's sound. It was a terrific song that she wrote and sang, and we vowed to try and find a place for it. The party was it. The reunion between Alec and Magnus was a lovely moment executed perfectly by Harry and Matt. The alley behind the Hunter's Moon with the gorgeous hanging lanterns is actually on our stage, but the romantic scope Hastings captured makes you swear they're outside. Small scenes like Izzy and Clary bonding over sisterhood are moments I lived for doing the show. Simon saying goodbye to Maia knowing he might not see her for a very long time is beautifully heartbreaking. When Jace tells Clary to keep his resurrection between them, one can feel the sense of foreboding ahead. Dom knew what was coming for Jace, and his seizure outside of the Hunter's Moon was just the right amount of disturbing to indicate that he was slowly becoming possessed. The idea of the wraith demons suddenly disappearing into a cave so they can drop from the ceiling and coalesce into a single female figure felt right for the grand entrance of Lilith, the queen of hell. At this point we knew Lilith would appear in season 3, but we had yet to be officially picked up for season three so we couldn't yet cast the actress who would play the part. Instead we cast a fine actress and covered her in goo so you wouldn't be able to distinguish her from next season, if we should be so lucky.

Up until this point we had heard positive rumblings about a potential season three but nothing had been officially announced. Although we were confident, we didn't know the number of episodes, and we definitely knew not to take anything for granted in this industry. They call it show business for a reason. Darren and I flew back to Toronto for the table read of 219 and 220, where we were bombarded with cast and crew gently asking if we'd heard anything yet. We had not. The network upfronts, held in New York, were happening at the same time, we assumed it would be announced then. Upfronts were an event held by every network to showcase and sell their upcoming shows for advertisers. On our way into the studio, we ran into Robert Kulzer and Margo Klewans from Constantine, headed to the airport on their way to New York. They too hadn't heard, but Robert didn't seem anxious. He had just watched the first five episodes of season 2b and was extremely complimentary. It was a warm moment in a relationship that started chillier. When we arrived, the first few times we met, I always felt he was skeptical of us. I assumed it was because of his strong relationship with the former showrunner, which I understood, but in this exchange there was nothing but mutual warmth and respect. We all crossed our fingers we'd hear about a pick-up soon.

After the table read we flew back to L.A. but there was still no renewal news when we landed. That was strange. The following day, a Friday, we went into the office to make final adjustments on the script and work on post-production for 216 and 217. The office was quiet with only support staff. While normally the writer's assistant would leave when the writers were finished, we kept Taylor on the payroll because of her expertise in all things Mortal Instruments. The depth of her knowledge had proven to be an invaluable resource not just for the writers but for the art department as well, and we didn't know if questions would arise during production on the last two episodes that we would need her to help answer.

The phone call came at noon from Jenn Gerstenblatt in New York, with McG, Mary Viola, Robert Kulzer, Margo Klewans and Matt Hastings already on the line. Before we picked up we knew this was probably the verdict, and we weren't wrong. Jenn's voice beamed with excitement as she told us we would be getting a twenty-episode season three. Many cheers and screams and "thank you's" could be heard. Zoe listened in on most of our calls and appeared in the doorway with a wide grin on her face. We did it. We were hired to board a ship on troubled waters and somehow managed to right that ship in a direction that the powers that be liked enough to spend sixty million dollars to produce twenty more hours. I was immensely relieved and deeply proud of the accomplishment. But I also knew our work was just beginning. The bar had been set. It was on us to now raise that bar and make the next season even better.

# SEASON THREE TO BE

Creatively I felt like we were in a good place knowing that we would be leaning heavily on City of Fallen Angels, the fourth book in The Mortal Instruments series and one of my favorites. Lilith was such an interesting, powerful villain who I couldn't wait to write and adapt for television. As a mother trying desperately to resurrect her dead child, she was achingly relatable. The Church of Talto would be a great location, but we also wanted to give her an elegant pied a terre that would show off her great taste and desires and help humanize her. Jace falling under her control as the Owl would be chilling and give Dom Sherwood the opportunity to stretch and do things as an actor he hadn't yet done before on the show. Even though Jonathan died, we wanted him to continue to haunt Jace in his dreams and hallucinations. We went about trying to secure Will Tudor for a few episodes, knowing we'd want to bring him back full time in 3b. Alisha Wainwright had proven to be as amazing as we thought she'd be in season 2, and we now wanted to make her a series regular in the show. This would mean giving her a nice raise and guaranteeing she'd be in at least seven of the ten episodes per season, which we supported wholeheartedly. Her availability now would no longer be a question mark. We wouldn't have to worry about her getting snatched up by another show and leaving us with no Maia. Jordan Kyle, Maia's ex-boyfriend and the werewolf who first turned her, would enter the shadow world in season three, befriending Simon like he did in the books, but not as a singer in the band. Our casting directors both in L.A. and Toronto had their work cut out for them as they began their search for Jordan and Lilith.

Lilith was a tough character to cast because we weren't looking for what the audience would expect, which was a kind of Cruella Devilla type bent on world domination. Our version of Lilith had a softer, more caring side to her that could easily slip into frightening anger when provoked. I received a facebook message from my old colleague Anna Hopkins, who I had worked with on DEFIANCE and was not only a great actor but a sweet human being. She was letting me know that she was auditioning for the role in Toronto and thought the character looked like she would be so fun to play. I saw her audition a few days later and she was as good as I expected, but I wondered if she was too young. For a woman who had been alive thousands of years, she looked surprisingly fresh and fabulous. Matt and Darren agreed, although we all loved her audition. We were curious what others thought and were shocked and wonderfully surprised when the network singled Anna out as their favorite. Even though I technically wasn't supposed to, I grabbed the phone and quickly dialed her up in Montreal. To this day I can still remember the delightful squeal she let out upon hearing the great news. Anna would be our Lilith.

The process of casting Jordan Kyle was longer and more arduous. Because of his difficult past full of reprehensible behavior, it was important that we cast someone who was extremely likeable and approachable. The audience needed to understand why Maia fell in love with him in the first place. We saw young men from all across the globe, but no one stood out like they usually do. Many were good, but we were striving for great. Jordan wouldn't appear until 304, so there was no rush. Chai Hansen's self-taped audition came through our Los Angeles casting director. Chai was half-Australian and half-Thai, with a face that was both handsome and incredibly warm and inviting. He lived in

Queensland, where he had taped his audition, and possessed the kind of laid-back spirit you'd expect from a surfer growing up on the Gold Coast. He had been a recurring character on THE HUNDRED and the casting folks at the network were big fans of his. Darren and I loved his look and vibe, but his self-taped audition was a bit raw and his accent at times made it difficult to understand him. Of course, we understood he wasn't being directed by anyone, and he was reading scenes that were taken completely out of context. Would he be markedly better "on the day" with a director helping him along? This was a question we constantly asked ourselves when casting roles. In the case of Chai, his persona was too great to pass up and we decided to pull the trigger.

Once production ended on season 2b and Matt Hastings had a moment to breathe after directing the epic two-parter, we got on the phone with Matt, Chris Hatcher and Doug McCullough to talk about the new sets we wanted to build for season three. Simon would move out of the boat basin and into an apartment he'd share with Jordan. While the Church of Talto acted as Lilith's home base in the first few episodes, we wanted to eventually give Lilith her own apartment that could actually move to different locations, a conceit that was set up in the book series with Magnus' apartment and one we felt we could deftly use with Lilith to continually keep her ahead of our Shadowhunters that were trying to track her down. And lastly, if we had space, we wanted to build a proper police bullpen space for Luke. The set in season one wasn't to our liking so we avoided the station in season two. But now that Ollie knew about the shadow world, we knew we would write more scenes with them together at work. With Magnus seeing clients again, we liked the idea of building an apothecary full of potions and things like lizard claws so we could see him at work. Matt wanted to continue to build out the Chinatown street outside of Hunter's Moon to avoid going on location in the dead of winter. The good news was that most of these sets didn't play in the premiere, so the art department would have plenty of time to build.

We had a month before the writer's room began on season three, and many positions in that room needed to be filled. Q would be returning as a Co-Executive Producer, essentially our number two. Jamie Gorenberg would also be back as a Co-Executive Producer. Pete Binswanger, who was there from the very beginning of season one, would return as well. After Taylor Mallory's phenomenal free-lance episode, we knew we wanted to hire her as a staff writer if we got a season three. That left four openings to fill. Agents and managers filled our e-mail boxes with submissions, many of which were awesome scripts. While we continued to work on post-production for the remaining episodes in season two, our days were spent poring over scripts and meeting writers. Casting a writer's room is similar to casting a group of actors. Chemistry is crucial. Not only did they have to be talented, able to write well and be articulate enough to pitch their ideas, they also needed to be people who we wouldn't mind hanging out with all day.

Once I knew season three was official, I immediately placed a call to a writer in Toronto, Aisha Porter Christie, who I had met through my sister-in-law Debbie in 2012. Debbie was involved with the Emmy college intern program and suggested I bring an intern onto the show I was currently working on, which was DEFIANCE. Aisha flew out from New York, where she was in film school at Columbia University. Born in Jamaica, Aisha was brimming with talent. She had written a spec pilot that I loved and was clearly ready for a career writing television. When we re-upped for Defiance season two, I was ready to bring her on staff, but I wasn't the showrunner. The talented Kevin Murphy had that role and was weary of hiring someone on the writing staff with such little experience. Instead, we hired her as a P.A., which would bring her back to Los Angeles and allow her to be in the writer's room as much as possible to learn as much as she could. Being a great writer didn't necessarily translate to being a great P.A., and Aisha was living proof of that. Aisha is one of the most real, grounded people you'll ever meet, so forcing a smile while serving food to hungry writers was far beyond her reach.

But she did manage to express her love for Y.A. genre shows, including a series on Freeform at the time called TWISTED. At the end of that season we mutually parted ways, but I knew our paths would cross again. Aisha returned to Toronto where she found work on the writing staff of ORPHAN BLACK and was currently writing on a Canadian show called FRANKIE SHAW. When I mentioned the possibility of coming back to L.A. to work on Shadowhunters, she seemed thrilled. She had been obsessed with the film THE MORTAL INSTRUMENTS back in 2012, going so far as to talk about it in the Defiance writer's room back in the day and encourage those who were interested to watch it. Now she had the chance to come back to Hollywood, the epicenter of the television industry, and work on the show that was based on the books. I told her to watch as much of season two as she could and quickly went about setting up a Skype meeting for her to meet the executives at the network.

With Michael Reisz and Zac Hug no longer with the show, we felt it was important to have an LGBTQ man on staff. The Malec relationship was a critical and popular part of the show, and as two straight men, Darren and I wanted the perspective of a gay man on the writing staff to help us make sure their journey felt authentic and truthful. Margo Klewans called us with a writer suggestion that she thought would be great for the show. Alex Schemmer was a former actor who was now a fantastic writer, penning several pilots as well as working on a season of MOZART IN THE JUNGLE. His pilot was terrific, full of funny, deep dialogue, and our meeting was even better. A Harvard graduate, Alex was clearly brilliant as well as extremely thoughtful. More quiet and introspective than the other writers on staff, we knew he would provide a necessary counterbalance and a perspective on the material that no one else had.

The Writer's Guild invited various showrunners to a mixer with diverse writers one evening at their headquarters in West Hollywood, and Darren and I decided to attend. Usually we read material and then met with the writer, so this was backwards for us, but it proved to be a great evening full of interesting conversations. Basically it was set up like speed dating, where each showrunner would sit at a table, and every ten minutes two or three writers would sit down before us and introduce themselves. We met many great people, but the one who stood out to us was Celeste Vasquez. She had come up as an assistant on THE VAMPIRE DIARIES, where she had co-written two freelance episodes. She had a wry wit that made me want to read her material. The next morning I called her manager for a script, and that night Darren and I read her spec YA pilot about a girl growing up in both the white and Hispanic worlds in L.A. It was terrific. We told her manager to have her watch as much of season 2 as she could and then come in for a meeting with us. She did, but it felt like her nerves got the best of her. Even though it was clear she was talented, her enthusiasm felt muted. Later her former boss on Vampire Diaries emailed us a long, glowing recommendation, an email that helped push us over the edge. Her potential was too strong to ignore.

Besides Q and Jamie, the rest of the staff were lower level writers who had little experience in a writer's room, so for that last slot we were looking for a mid-level writer to help even things out. Brian Milikin came up on HAVEN and was coming off of TEEN WOLF, both shows sharing something in common with Shadowhunters. His sample was submitted by his agent, and Darren and I both responded. We had a wonderful meeting and felt like he understood the show well. His talent and experience, combined with his calm, easy-going demeanor, would fit well with the group. We were quickly sold.

Writers weren't the only people we needed to hire. We also needed to replenish the support staff, who were either being promoted or moving on to greener pastures. Zoe had been a showrunner's assistant for two seasons now and was more than ready to take the next step as a writer's assistant. She recommended a few people she knew who would be interested in replacing her, one of them a current assistant at Verve (the same literary agency that Zoe worked at before Shadowhunters) who was a huge fan of the book series. Many burgeoning writers, including myself back in the day, begin their careers working at agencies as a way to learn about the business, hone their admin skills, and most importantly make vital networking contacts that will help them find their next job. We met Claire Hupy during her lunch hour. She was clearly smart, a year out of the USC screenwriting program with an energy and enthusiasm that was infectious, as well as a vast knowledge of the Mortal Instrument book series. We asked to read a writing sample, as we did with all support staff candidates we were interested in hiring. We understood people weren't after this job for the money. They were looking for more of a learning experience, and we were interested in acting as genuine mentors. It was important that their work was good enough to merit the time we'd invest in teaching them the ropes and hopefully championing their careers. Claire's script, as I expected, was terrific, and we hired her the following day.

Jeff, our loyal P.A., would replace the talented Joey Elkins as script coordinator. That meant we needed to hire a new P.A., the keeper of all things food related, which as I said before was a vital position that if handled poorly could affect the morale of the entire writing staff. Zoe mentioned that Margo's former assistant and a smart, rising executive at Constantin, James Madjeski, was interested. I was initially worried that he would quickly grow resentful fetching lunch every day, but after meeting with James our concerns evaporated. He wanted to be a writer, not an executive, and felt that this unique situation at Shadowhunters where the showrunners were interested in hearing his thoughts and mentoring his writing career was worth giving up that career and starting anew in another.

In between our steady stream of meetings and post-production sessions, we were also in search of new offices with a writer's room that didn't also double as a kitchen. Zoe, Darren and I trekked across the neighborhood touring office spaces with our pal at the network, Sheryl Fountain. Even though Darren and I lived on the west side, we were mixing and coloring the show in Hollywood and Burbank, so it made sense to stay in that neighborhood. Sadly, that neighborhood seemed to be deteriorating daily, the homelessness problem reaching crisis levels. Eventually we settled into offices with a nice writer's room and offices for every writer but situated on a depressing piece of land with barred windows that looked out on a very dreary street. Those offices would only be temporary until the swanky suites across the street opened up in October.

The week before the room began, Darren and I took a few days off to clear our heads and attempt not to think about anything in any way related to Shadowhunters. My wife and I drove up the coast to Montecito and stayed at our favorite hotel for a few nights. The only Shadowhunters business was a conference call with the network, Constantin and Wonderland regarding directors.

We knew we wanted to bring back many directors from season two. The question was whether they were available. Talented directors work all the time, so pinning them down can be difficult. Matt Hastings ran point on hiring directors, but unlike season two, we would have input as well. Matt was calling in from France, where he was vacationing with his family. The network and Wonderland had several people they wanted us to meet, including Emile Levisetti and Ari Sandel. Director meetings would begin the following week and continue through the month, with Matt joining in over FaceTime sipping rose on the balcony of his villa (true story).

On the Friday before Memorial Day weekend and then the first day of the writer's room, I drove out to Hollywood to check out the new offices, which were now mostly moved into. Claire was there training with Zoe before her official first day. I took them out for sushi at Sugar Fish. We celebrated Zoe's promotion into the writer's room, which was a true accomplishment. And I enjoyed the calm before the storm that I knew was soon to come - hopefully a perfect storm of a new collection of creative personalities coming together in a single room to create amazing stories. I was looking forward to the thunder and lightning, but I knew once it began I would miss the peaceful quietude.

# WRITERS UNITE

The first few weeks of writing a new season of television were usually fun and relaxed because the pressure and distraction of production hasn't yet reared its ugly head. The writing side of the job occupied most of my days and the use of our collective boundless imaginations felt enormously liberating. Maybe it was because we hired these writers ourselves, but their chemistry with each other felt particularly strong. They were each totally different people from different parts of the world with entirely different perspectives on life, but their creative flow felt organic, and good ideas were being born all day long. It was nice to see Q in a leadership role among the fellow writers. He had never been a Co-EP before, but you'd never know it. The staff had a great deal of affection for him as he expertly curated all of their collective ideas into the awesome pitches he would deliver to me and Darren.

Those first days back we talked a lot about ways to intersect the mundane world with the shadow world. That dynamic had always been one of my favorite parts of the show, but it was easy to lose sight of it when the stories primarily took place between characters within the shadow world. That's why Ollie would be a great story engine for Luke, and Isabelle wanting to date a mundane would throw her in the mundane world more than ever. Simon's continual pull toward his mundane family would grow more complicated as the season went on and would sadly prove to be untenable. A newly de-runed Maryse returning to New York forced to live the life of a mundane would pull all the Lightwoods into that world in fun and unexpected ways.

Eating lunch together was always a great way for a staff to get to know each other, when they weren't working and were simply hanging out. On most of the shows I've worked on, the writers' lunches are paid for by the studio. This keeps all the writers in the office during the lunch hour rather than have them wander out into the outside world where they could disappear for up to 90 minutes if the restaurant service was bad enough. As we were gearing up for season three, Zoe informed me that in the past their lunches were only paid for during production, not before. I called Jayne Bieber, the head of physical production who had always been nice and pragmatic with me. I pleaded my rehearsed speech about how much a paid lunch would help our productivity and before I could finish my sentence she said yes. Yet another example of how positive my experience was with all things Freeform.

During their break in production, many of the cast members made pilgrimages to the writer's offices bearing all kinds of goodies. Before the holidays Kat came in with a basket of home baked cookies for the writers. Alisha visited after returning to L.A. from Toronto with her baked creations. In June, Isaiah and Harry stopped by with Isaiah's mom and countless boxes of donuts. Emeraude swept in one afternoon with bottles of wine and champagne. It was always great to see them away from the set when they were their most relaxed. They were always so nice to us and the writers, and it was great to see their eyes steal glances at the scrawl-filled white boards looking for any hint as to what was coming down the line for their character.

Most of the season arcs for each character were created in those first two weeks. Clary would be dealing with Jace's increasingly bizarre behavior while also being forced to keep the secret of his resurrection from the family around her.

Eventually she would end up sacrificing her freedom and life to save him and stop Lilith. Magnus would be stripped of his High Warlock of Brooklyn title and the political responsibilities that came with it, but instead of wallowing in self-pity he'd embrace his capitalistic swagger and start seeing clients full blown. I wanted to dial up his wardrobe, hair and make-up back to the levels of season one, with a broader, wilder David Bowie/Freddie Mercury vibe. The quippy comedic Magnus from season one would reemerge as he and Alec settled into their form of cute domesticity. Of course, their bliss would be interrupted by Lilith's evil ways and they'd each have to sacrifice themselves in their own way to save Jace and defeat Lilith.

As the acclaimed leader of the New York Institute who helped to take down Valentine, Alec would be dealing with the politics between the New York Institute and their relationship with the Clave in Alicante, all the while concerned about the mental health of his parabatai. Simon would be dealing with his mark of Cain and the destruction that lay in its wake, and eventually come to the sad realization that he had to completely sever ties with his mother in order to protect her. Isabelle would not only become the new weapons master, but she'd also become romantically involved with a mundane and realize it's too dangerous to be involved with anyone outside of the shadow world, paving the way for her future relationship with our favorite vampire. Luke would now have to deal with his mundane police partner knowing all there is to know about the shadow world, and eventually succumb to her close proximity to the greater demon better known as Lilith. Maia would be dealing with the return of Jordan Kyle and all the painful memories she spent all these years trying to suppress. The big surprise was Raphael digging up poor Heidi and turning her into a vampire to see if she was a daylighter. It was going to be an exciting season for the show.

After two weeks, on a blindingly bright summer morning, Darren and I and Claire with her laptop (to take notes after the pitch) trekked out to Burbank and into a conference room to take Freeform, Constantin and Wonderland into the dark recesses of season 3a. The blinds would have to be closed for this pitch. They thoroughly enjoyed it and had good notes to make it better. Originally Lilith was fascinated with the mundane world after being in Edom for so long, and spent more time enjoying things like fashion and gourmet dining. Jenn Gerstenblatt wisely thought it was best to stay from those tropes and focus more on her relationships with our characters, which was smart and taken to heart. We left elated, and before heading back to the offices, we went out to the world renown Bob's Big Boy for lunch to celebrate.

301 aka "On Infernal Ground" came together very quickly, in the room and on the page. It was darker in tone than anything we had previously done on the show, and more mature. Lilith was a joy to write. The scene in the nursery between Lilith and the kind-hearted nurse Tim Metcafle is a personal favorite. Her tenderly told story about her broken relationship with Adam (as in Adam and Eve) and her inability to have children of her own felt like an interesting, sympathetic introduction to this dark, evil character. Anna Hopkins was even better than we thought she'd be, and Randal Edwards as Tim was an awesome surprise. Matt Hastings had worked with Randal years ago, so we knew he would be good, but we didn't know how good. Matt masterfully directed the scene as he did the entire episode. Her long, black nails resting on the glass of the nursery full of beautiful newborn babies is an indelible image that stays with you.

While writing the script in our dark office, Darren and I had a heated debate about the Queen of Edom's razor-sharp fingernails. We both loved the idea of her drawing blood from her possessed disciples and using that blood as a kind of rebirthing placenta-like fluid to resurrect dead Jonathan lying secretly under the altar. A knife was suggested but it felt too mundane. A sharp rock was brought up but that felt too impersonal and real. I brought up the nail as an extension of herself and her true appearance as a slimy, slithering wraith demon with razor sharp claws. Darren thought it would look cheesy and possibly goofy. I thought it would look cool. As we often did when we were at an impasse on the show, we let Matt Hastings cast the final vote.

The violence in the episode was more real and visceral than anything we had previously done on the show. I worried about moving too deep into the dark shadows where it would no longer be appropriate for some of our audience, but I also knew that if we were going to tell stories about the Queen of Edom and her desire to stop at nothing to bring her son back, those stories had to display the darkness in her soul. Writing the violence on the page was one thing, but seeing it on the screen in all its bloody gore worried me even more. It was extremely well done - so well done that it all felt terrifyingly realistic.

The visual effect shots of Alicante, particularly the opening shot after the credits soaring over the city of glass, are nothing less than spectacular. The attention to detail, including the flowing water fountains, is incredible. The artists at Folks delivered the goods in season two, every episode seemingly more elaborate than the previous one, and now they had taken their artistry to even greater heights. Clary battling the wraith demon in the dark marketplace is jaw-dropping, as is Luke the wolf arriving to save Ollie. The wolves were particularly difficult and expensive to execute, and they nailed it here. The on-screen dedication at the end of the episode is to the Folks artist Simon Jacques, who passed away only a few months earlier.

The locations and sets continued to feel more complex and sophisticated. The Church of Talto as an abandoned hotel ballroom from a different era, complete with bandstands on stage and a decrepit roof above (created by Folks VFX) that leaked eerie moonlight, was both ominous and sadly nostalgic. Isabelle's new weapons room was a terrific addition, full of cool looking swords, knives and other goodies. The sliding open confession booth was a fun place to store her weapons. Originally there was a cross on the etched glass but after seeing it in the director's cut, Darren and I worried the religious iconography took the audience out of the fantasy world and opted for Folks to erase it with their magic visual effect wand. Jace's bedroom was enlarged and reconceived, knowing we'd be spending a lot of time there in season three with poor Jace haunted by his series of bloody, disturbing dreams.

The only real lightness in the episode was evident in the Simon story, the poor vampire trapped in the Seelie Court where he's forced to serenade the Queen while being massaged and served blood by her fairies. Of course, that story eventually grows darker when he's branded with the Mark of Cain, but even that strange ceremony, as depraved as it is, is also absurdly funny. Alberto was magnificent in that scene, especially since he was playing his part in front of a body double. Lola Flaherty wasn't available due to her shooting schedule on THE HUNDRED. She filmed her side of their conversation on a green screen stage weeks later and then was seamlessly cut together, the visual effects perfecting the illusion. We were ecstatic when we saw Matt's director's cut.

Because of the darkness in 301, we wanted 302 to be lighter and more playful. Centering the main story around Magnus and the warlock community would certainly lend a whimsical tone to the show no matter how grave the stakes would become. We also wanted to lean back into the romantic and relationship stories that we had abandoned the last few episodes in the rush to save the world. At the core of the show and book series, the concept that love knows no boundaries has always been a central theme, and one so many of us can relate to. The idea of Jace wanting to take Clary out on a proper date felt so wonderfully pure, and the accidental double date between them and Simon and Maia would be a great opportunity for comedy, something we always strive to lace through the stories whenever appropriate. I longed for Jace to tell Clary and remind the audience why he thinks she's so special. I knew some would criticize it as being too earnest, but I loved the idea of Jace pouring his feelings out in this beautiful monologue where Clary could only respond with tears of love welling in her eyes. The chemistry between Kat and Dom was apparent from their first moment together in season one, and we were eager to mine it more in season three.

Magnus and Alec and the cute but awkward domesticity that was now a part of their relationship were scenes that I and the audience were dying to experience. This was a priority for 302 as well as the rest of season three. Maia and Simon, also in a "taboo" relationship thanks to the whole vampire/werewolf dynamic, was a relationship I was looking forward to exploring. Alberto and Alisha were magnetic together, their characters' ease and love for one another palpable in the most comfortable way. We knew we had to exploit that as much as we could early in the season, knowing that as soon as Jordan Kyle came into the picture, things would quickly get complicated. Lilith would continue to bring the darkness, but the light, buoyant nature of the other stories would help balance it all out and lend the show a dynamic that the somber "On Infernal Ground" sorely lacked.

We knew we wanted to introduce the new High Warlock of Brooklyn in 302 aka "The Powers That Be", and a warlock party at his mansion felt like the right place to do it. Lorenzo Rey would be bigger than life, broad and funny, and a welcome addition to the Shadow World as well as a foil and rival of our dear Magnus. We knew that Javier Munoz, who was currently on Broadway as Hamilton in the hit musical, was a big fan of the show based on his Twitter account. Matt Hastings met him in New York for coffee after seeing the play and brought up the notion of being on the show. Javier was more than enthusiastic, and when the role of Lorenzo Rey came up, we knew he'd be awesome. We told him that while he would begin in 302, if all went well, we would love for him to recur throughout the series. His performance in 302 proved he fit well in show, and we would go on to use him many more times in season 3.

Pete Binswanger brought his usual comedic skills to his script, but I must admit, the broad, over-the-top tone concerned me. Even though it was funny, it felt more season one than season two. Because the tone was different than what Darren and I had done before on the show, we deliberated over the script more than usual, and in the end, Pete delivered one of the most memorable episodes of the show. It was one of the few episodes where the Malec story was the "A" story, the main story where they were the characters who got to solve the mystery of the leyline corruption and eventually save the day. Peter Deluise, returning after the phenomenal job he did on 215, had a lot of experience directing comedy, much of it broader than we were used to. For the warlock party he wanted the waiters to wear white colonial wigs, but we felt with Javier Munoz in the scene, the wink to Hamilton for those in the know was simply too on the nose. We were worried that Alec and Magnus sneaking into Lorenzo's house to investigate the leyline corruption bordered on Buster Keaton/slapstick, but Peter managed to ground it in a way that pulled out the humor of both of the actors in the best way. I never considered Alec to be really funny until this episode. Matt Daddario's comedic skills surprised all of us and made us want to write more humor into the character as we moved forward.

The challenge for Darren and I was that his director's cut was eleven minutes over the allotted 42-minute running time. Directors usually never cut entire scenes in their director's cut because they want to deliver the script as shot to the showrunners. Peter's cut delivered all the moments and more in the dense script. Now it was up to us to get it to time. This required quickening the pace throughout the episode, including deleting many lines within scenes or deleting them all together. The editor Karen Castaneda proved how talented and patient she was as we sat in the editing bay with her and continued to chop away, cut after cut. Linday Wolfington's songs elevated the emotional resonance even more than usual. After all is said and done, "The Powers That Be" was a welcome reprieve from the darkness of 301 and easily ranks as the funniest episode of the series.

The premiere of season 2B was coming up soon and I was excited about watching and tweeting the show again live with the writing staff. Our post producer Marc Kahn also happened to be an expert at party planning and suggested having the premiere party at a cool Mexican restaurant downtown that his friend owned. Our new assistant Claire was thrown into the fire as a party planner as well and ended up doing a great job. Because the 5pm live broadcast was too early for guests to make it downtown, we scheduled it around the 8pm west coast airing. It was a festive occasion and an opportunity for the new writers to meet many of the people involved in the making of the show. I made another playlist that no one could hear. Kat, Alberto, Harry, Isaiah and Alisha all made it out. They all seemed to be enjoying their time off. They had yet to receive 301 so I breezily filled them in on what we had come up with so far. Alberto was thrilled about Simon finally getting the Mark of Cain and the problems it would create. When I told him he'd be singing another original song in the premiere, a huge smile swept across his face. Once again, I slipped out on the early side while the party was still raging, eager to hop on twitter and scroll through the fandom's reaction to 211.

# SAN DIEGO

During our days on SMALLVILLE, we attended the world-famous San Diego Comic-Con twice. The first time we were writers on staff, given the day off to go down and support our showrunners Al and Miles, who were on a panel with several of the actors. Darren and I drove down in our car together, fighting the massive traffic. The panel was held in one of the huge auditoriums, and the spectacle of it all was overwhelming. As a kid I went to a comic book convention in Anaheim, but this was the big leagues. Walking across the packed floor, checking out the various displays, I was overwhelmed with claustrophobia and nausea due to the waves of body odor coming at me from seemingly every direction, and vowed to never return. In season 8, when we were named showrunners along with Kelly Souders and Brian Peterson, we were required to go, and each of us was picked up at our homes by a chauffeured car that drove us to Union Station, where we took a train down to San Diego, picked up by another chauffeured car, and were driven to our hotel. It was a one hundred- and eighty-degrees different experience. We did a panel in one of those massive auditoriums with Justin Hartley, Erica Durance, and Allison Mack. Afterwards we did several interviews, some of which you can see online now, where we tried not to embarrass ourselves. It was an exhilarating day that gave me a newfound appreciation for the madness.

Because Shadowhunters was currently airing, this experience would be unique. The fans and press would not only want to talk about the upcoming season three but also about season 2b and how it was unfolding. Since we had no footage yet for season 3, we had cut together a one-minute sizzle-reel of the last three episodes of season 2b to get the crowd pumped before our panel. After work on a Wednesday, Darren and I shared a car that drove us straight to San Diego and our hotel. In the lobby we met Matt Hastings, back from his European vacation, for a drink at the hotel bar. I thought I recognized a few folks from the cast of STITCHERS, who were doing a panel tomorrow as well. We struck up a conversation, and before I knew it, Kat, Alberto, Dom and Matt swept into the bar, Alberto having flown straight here from Ireland where he was on holiday. They all seemed to be in good spirits, excited to be at the Comic-Con and eager to get back to work in just a few short weeks. It was great to see everyone, and we hung out for a bit before I excused myself to get some sleep. It was going to be a big day tomorrow.

The following morning, a hair and make-up person arrived at my room to do their thing. This was always horribly awkward for me. My face shows the scars of years of teenage acne and I have always been terribly self-conscious, especially in these circumstances. The woman was sweet, here from New York to do the hair and make-up of various attendees of the con. Afterwards I met Darren and Matt down in the lobby, and we hopped in a van that would take us to the Hilton Bayfront Hotel, where several panels were being held. When we arrived, we were greeted by our Freeform publicity friends who ushered us to a large room where the rest of the cast and their various reps were waiting for the panel. I spent some time with Harry, Emeraude and Isaiah, who weren't at our impromptu hotel party last night. Isaiah brought his teenage daughter, which I of course found wonderfully touching. I met the many managers and agents and executives who were associated with the show that I had never met before. While our obligation was the panel and the press afterwards, the cast's day was filled with interviews from morning to night. The Stitchers team filed into the room after their panel which meant we were now up.

We were led down a series of halls and into the backstage area connected to the massive hall. I couldn't help but think back on our days playing The Troubadour, where we sat excited backstage listening to the buzz and anticipation of the crowd. This was like that times a thousand. As the sizzle-reel played on the big screen in the hall, we could hear the howls and screams from the excited crowd. The cast craned their necks to try and look up at the screen, the first time they had seen any of the upcoming footage. Our names were called one by one and we all rushed into the glaring spotlight, staring out at what looked like endless rows of people. We announced a few major spoilers for season three, including the arrival of Lilith and Jordan and the welcoming news that Maia was now going to be a series regular on the show. I gave a shout-out to the writers, who had all taken the day off to come down and support us and who I could see were all sitting together. Afterwards we took a series of photos backstage with Karey Burke, who was there with her daughter, rooting us on. She had always been nothing but supportive to us, and it was good to see her.

The speed-dating press interaction awaited us in a bright ballroom. Darren and I were teamed with Matt, and like New York, we went table to table answering questions from four or five different journalists at each table, iPhones pointed at us recording our every word. It was both intimidating and exhilarating. Unlike New York, these journalists had seen our work. Most were extremely complimentary. A few book lovers were less than thrilled with the changes we'd made from the source material, but they all presented insightful questions and were a joy to interact with.

After saying our goodbyes to the cast, Darren, Matt and I took a quick walk across the main floor, taking in the sights and sounds and odors. This was Matt's first time at the convention, and he was in awe like we were our first time. A young teenage girl and her father politely stopped us for a picture. She was a huge Shadowhunters fan and had seen the panel earlier in the day. The awestruck look on her face as she gazed up at us gave me the best kind of goosebumps. The show meant so much to her. Our work had touched her deeply. It was a beautiful reminder of how blessed I was to do what I do. We met up with an old friend of Matt's, and the four of us quickly slipped out and made our way through the packed streets and into a wonderful seafood restaurant, where we celebrated the day. Matt was off to a party, hanging out for the rest of the weekend at the convention, while we jumped in our car for the drive back to L.A. We had work the next morning, but at this point it was hard to call it work. It was truly a joy.

# WHAT LIES BENEATH

The timing of when to reveal Jace was the Owl merited quite a bit of discussion in the writer's room. Many writers worried that if the audience knew he was the Owl but the shadowhunters did not, it would make our heroes feel less than smart. As a fan of suspense over mystery, I argued that as long as we managed the plot so there was no way the shadowhunters could know it was Jace, the audience's knowledge would invest them even more in the outcome and how it would affect all the characters. After debating the positives and negatives, we decided to reveal Jace to the audience at the end of 303 and to the Shadowhunters at the end of 306. Basically, if one looked at the ten-episode season as one feature film, the first reveal would be at the end of the first act.

The concept of The Owl came about in that first week in the room. When Q explained that the owl was a symbol for Satan in Luciferian worship and was linked to death, ruin and destruction in many middle eastern cultures, I thought it was the perfect construct to hide Jace while he went on his rampage infecting and possessing innocent, good-hearted people. Matt Hastings, the prosthetics team and the costume department created a look that was both unique to the show and utterly terrifying. It wasn't the easiest thing to fit into for Dom, but he was a trooper. For the initial mold to create the mask, he had to be completely still for two hours breathing only through a straw. If I didn't ask him about it when we were up in Toronto for the table read, he would have never uttered a word. Dom was the consummate professional.

303 aka "What Lies Beneath" was built around the hunt for the Owl and Jace believing the Owl was Jonathan. This would maximize the impact of the reveal at the end of the episode while giving the show a strong narrative drive. The frightening appearances of Jonathan would make Jace and the audience believe he could very well be right, only to discover later that they were hallucinations.

After setting up Raphael and his mysterious captive in the premiere, we wanted to reveal that the poor girl getting burned in the basement was Heidi and that she was hellbent on finding her sire aka Simon Lewis. Her escape at the end would be a terrific cliff-hanger into the next episode. Raphael's relationship with his sister Rosa, set up back in 209 and 212, would be paid off here with her sad passing. David Castro gives a heartbreaking performance throughout the episode; the scene between him and Isabelle is next level. The writing, the performances, the directing, and that song, is Shadowhunters at its best. Emeraude makes you feel Izzy's concern and compassion deep in your soul.

The bullpen set makes its debut in this episode in a terrific scene between Luke and Ollie where Ollie explains she's only told one other person, her girlfriend Sam. Alexandra Ordolis gives the character a naturalness that feels totally effortless. Luke struggles with his allegiance to his wolfpack and his loyalty to Simon in a tug and pull story that allows Isaiah to play both an inner strength and a raw vulnerability. The scene at the end in the boat basin when he is forced to evict Simon is a wonderful display of subtext, Isaiah's physicality playing his side of the scene instead of words.

The return of Maryse Lightwood with the news that she was being deruned and exiled to Alicante was ripe with dramatic possibilities and a few humorous opportunities as well. Nicola Correia-Damude had blown us away in

208 and 214 and we were eager to bring her back into the fold. The idea of a family dinner that turns out to be just Alec, Magnus and Maryse was the kind of sub-plot I loved on the show. Like the Alec and Magnus date in 206, it was a collection of scenes on one set that was all about character and emotion without relying on any outside plot devices. Alec anxiously cooking stew for his Mom with Magnus is one of my favorite scenes of the series. A guilty Maryse coming clean and telling her son the truth about her horrible past with Valentine is heartbreaking. And the end, when Maryse thanks Magnus "for loving my boy," gives me chills every time. Alex Schemmer, the writer of the episode, said his boyfriend's mother spoke those same words to him and it always stayed with him. The truth of his experience shined through in that moment, evidenced by the flood of messages I've received from parents of LGBTQ children all over the world who said that scene and Maryse's Lightwood acceptance of her gay son had a direct influence on the way they treated their own child. Bravo, Alex.

We knew Alex was talented based on his sample we had read, but we didn't know how well he'd write an episode of Shadowhunters… until we read his writer's draft for 303. Holy cow it was amazing. His dialogue was fantastic, and his scene work was exceptionally strong. As a former actor his writing was especially intuitive and honest, and I found myself continually impressed page after page. Darren and I had very few notes, all of which he expertly executed with grace and aplomb. Amanda Row directed another solid episode, but the explosive magic we expected wasn't there. Of course, there were terrific moments throughout, especially the mind-blowing Jace and Jonathan face-off in a room full of mirrors that remains one of the most interesting action sequences of the series. Obviously, the story and script were completely different, the episode more of a procedural than 218 with less emphasis on emotion and more on plot. We also had a new editor, Erik Presant, cutting the show. He was extremely talented but there was naturally a learning curve for anyone new. The show came out okay. Not our best, but definitely not our worst.

The writer's room delivered a particularly strong story for 304 aka "Thy Soul Instructed." The introduction of Jordan was a fun reprieve from the darkness of 303. Chai Hansen had flown in the day before the table read, and even he would admit his performance that day was a bit wobbly, but on camera he was terrific. Charming, funny, and frightening at the end, he was Jordan in our eyes. Utilizing Heidi, a character who was already part of the show canon, as the villain of the episode, would make the audience more invested in the story than if the villain was a stranger. Darren and I always felt that new villains who weren't part of our canon didn't carry the same emotional impact that villains we already knew did. The great news about Shadowhunters seasons 2a and 2b was that Valentine and Jonathan acted as the primary villains in almost every episode. When they weren't the villains, we liked to bring back characters who had already been introduced in the show. Hence Iris Rouse as the feline party crasher in 208 and Kaylee the revenge-seeking Seelie in 213. Heidi seeking revenge against Raphael was something the audience would understand after what he did to her, and the best villains were always the ones viewers could relate to even though they might disagree with their methods.

Jace questioning his mental health was important to me on a personal level as mental illness was an issue I had grown up with. Various family members of mine have suffered from this illness that carries an enormous amount of stigma, even today. As a child, my Mom volunteered at a mental health clinic in Los Angeles and I often heard the stories of her various clients. My stepfather was the President of the L.A. County Mental Health Association up until his recent retirement. I liked the message that if one did suffer from mental health issues, it was okay to be out in the open with it and seek help, even if you were a masculine soldier like Jace Herondale. The scene between Jace and Luke in the Jade Wolf when Luke speaks about Jace's mother's mental health struggles moved me deeply, both on screen and on the page.

Jamie Gorenberg penned another great script, and Emile Levisetti's spot-on direction made it even greater. We had never worked with Emile before, but he was clearly accomplished. The sequence on the rooftop with Heidi and Raphael was fantastic, bolstered by the terrific VFX that made the viewer believe they were outside on top of a building rather than on our sound stage. The fight between

Leo, the poor phlebotomist-turned-vampire, and Clary and Izzy was extraordinary. We cast Jesse Camacho as Leo not only because he was a great actor whose audition was strong, but we wanted to show representation of all types on the show, including size. Some worried he would be too comedic. He was a funny guy, but we insisted he could pull off both the humor and the terror when he later became a vampire. All the performances were particularly strong. Tessa Mossey continued to bring Heidi to life in the best, most bizarre way possible. Emeraude's pain at discovering that Raphael was behind her torture was absolutely heartbreaking. Dom was brilliant and believable, both as Jace and the Owl under Lilith's control. Anna Hopkins was again phenomenal, continuing to add layers and complexities to Lilith. In the original story Lilith made Jace sleep with her, but the powers that be deemed that too icky, so we settled on a deep French kiss. They were probably right.

305 aka "Stronger Than Heaven" picked up literally right where 304 ended. The last scene in 304, where Lilith arrived at Magnus' apartment looking to use his services, was a binge-worthy push-off that forced the viewer to tune in next week to figure out what the hell she was doing there. After doing two procedural shows in a row, 305 would lean into the mythology more by Clary trying to summon the Angel Ithuriel with Cleophas's help. We had longed to bring back Lisa Berry since her terrific performances in season 2, and this show would give us the opportunity. The twist that Lilith would end up killing Ithuriel before he could reveal her identity added to the power and danger of Lilith, especially in her beastly demonic form which Folks VFX masterfully created. After a lighter story in 304, Magnus and Alec were at the forefront with Alec discovering Magnus' precious box with mementos from all the people he's been in love with over the years. This would propel them into a fight that would last several episodes. We knew the subject of Magnus' immortality would eventually rear its ugly head like it did in the books and were always excited by their relationship facing dramatic conflicts even though we knew many fans didn't share our enthusiasm.

Simon learning about Jordan's real identity was always scheduled to happen here, with Jace playing an instrumental role in the discovery. The supermarket scene from the books was one of my favorites and I tried to insert it into the story, but I knew the reality of production made it too difficult. When shooting on location, ideally you want to craft several scenes there so the shoot will take up an entire day and not just four hours. The idea of Simon performing another song was something we pushed from the beginning, and the story of his gig getting cancelled by his fake manager would add a mystery that Jace would throw himself into solving in order to give him something to do while he was benched from his shadowhunter duties. Dom and Alberto have always had great chemistry, and whenever we could put the two actors together in a scene or a story we rejoiced. The mystery would also pay off nicely when you found out it was Jordan, who was just trying to look out for him. Sam Hollander's "Michelangelo" might be my favorite song of his collection, and it serves as a wonderful soundtrack when Lilith finally "drugs" Jace into submission.

Brian Millikin deserves an apology after we changed "a sliver of Clary's soul" into "a sliver of Clary's hair" during our rewrite of his script. Darren and I were grinding with the ethereal nature of stealing someone's soul. It felt too fantastical for our taste, but the network, after reading our draft, liked the soul thing better so we reverted back to the original conceit. Of course, Brian was his usual gracious self, never once complaining or giving us a sidelong "I told you so" glance. He was a total pro and one of the kindest, most warm-hearted people I've ever worked with. Geoff Shotz, a former camera operator who Matt had worked with before, did a wonderful job directing this epic episode. It was both visually stunning and deeply moving. John Rakich and his team found a remarkable location for Luke's farmhouse that Cleophas was currently staying in, and the "Three Acres Farm" signage added a nice Easter egg for book fans. He also found a fantastic restaurant for Izzy and Charlie's date.

The character of Underhill had his first real scene in the series with Alec, a scene that was actually originally shot in 215 between Aline and Alec. Because of time, it didn't fit in that episode, and we pondered releasing it on social media as a deleted scene. But I felt if released as a deleted scene it could potentially send the message that we didn't think it was important enough to be on the show, which was the farthest thing from the truth. I knew how important it was for a gay shadowhunter to reach out to Alec to tell him he was a role model for shadowhunters like him. We rewrote the scene for Underhill and it remains one of my favorites of the series. Steve Byers is a phenomenal actor, and when we originally approached him about the role, he worried the part might be too small and inconsequential for an actor with his talent and experience. I convinced him that 303 and 304 were just setting him up for the two episodes that would follow, and he happily trusted us and agreed to step into the shadow world. How lucky we were.

After all the money we spent on 305, episode 306 aka "A Window Into An Empty Room" had to be significantly under budget, shot in only seven days opposed to our normal eight day schedule. One of the stories I liked best from the books was Simon being stalked by his fellow bandmate Maureen, who had become a vampire after he drank her blood and Camille turned her. In the show Heidi would basically play the role of Maureen the stalker with a different origin story and agenda. I loved the idea that she was obsessed with his music and listened to it all the time, assuming they belonged together since he was technically her sire. FATAL ATTRACTION is one my favorite thrillers, and this story played with that conceit because we, the audience, could sympathize with her while also sympathizing with Simon.

The episode would be inexpensive to produce, basically taking place all on our sets. The story would center around Maryse returning to New York City as a mundane. It was full of awesome dramatic and emotional potential and also gave us the chance again to stay on our sets, with the majority of that story taking place at the Hunter's Moon complete with a little family party that involved all of Maryse's children. Simon would be there to try to protect Maia from Heidi, and Luke would show up as well for his chance to flirt with his secret crush Maryse.

Book fans would be happy to see their beloved Brother Zacariah at last in a powerful scene with Magnus and Clary. We knew he didn't speak in the books but rather communicated telepathically. Darren and I worried this would come off as inherently goofy, and auditioned actors who actually spoke. Jonathan Ho rose to the top with his boyish innocence combined with eyes that appeared to be wiser beyond his years. With the silver streak in his hair and his hooded wardrobe, I was all in. We had him do the scene both speaking and simply looking at the characters while the script supervisor read his lines, which would give us a choice in the editing room.

After his nasty fight with Magnus, Alec would get drunk and bump into Underhill at - where else - the Hunter's Moon. There was much discussion about how far their flirtations should go. My instinct was that drunken Alec should make a grave mistake and lock lips with the man, but I was luckily persuaded by my colleagues that the Malec fans would riot. The flirting was enough to make Alec feel terribly guilty, as well as protect Underhill and not turn him into the shadow world's most hated man. Crisis averted. The last act of the episode is chalk full of major moments, including Ollie's possession and the discovery by our heroes that their beloved Jace is actually the Owl. I wasn't thrilled ending the show on the Jace reveal, considering viewers already knew what was going on, but it was the only ending that truly felt like an ending.

Aisha Porter Christie delivered an awesome draft just as we expected. Her writing was crisp, full of smart, snappy dialogue. She was also able to execute our notes elegantly and with precision, a skill not every TV writer possesses but one that is absolutely necessary if you want to rise through the ranks. Because we were the ones who uprooted her from her successful career in Canada, I was often concerned that she wasn't having a good time and would rather be back home. Luckily for me, soon after she started the job, she formed close friendships with the entire staff, especially Taylor and Celeste, and her performance on the show was extraordinary. Alexis Ostrander directed and did a solid job, especially given her budget and time constraints. The performances were all fantastic.

The fancy offices across the street had finally opened up and were waiting for us with open arms, but a quick polling of the staff showed that they felt that it was better to stay here. All the writers and support staff had their own offices, which wouldn't be the case in the fancy digs. Some people would have to share. And while the offices were indeed depressing and on a decrepit piece of land, we had all grown accustomed to it and didn't want to start over in a new environment. It was the devil we knew. This would be our home for the remainder of the show.

# NORTHERN LIGHTS

In the beginning of August, Darren and I made our now customary trip to the Great White North to help launch season 3a. At the airport in L.A. before we boarded, I received a call from Q, who filled me in on the latest ideas for 307. As a showrunner, one of the toughest things for me was to respond honestly to material I didn't like. I consider myself a positive, affable person who avoids conflict whenever I can, so having to say to someone who's worked their ass off that you don't like their work is hard for me. Of course, this wasn't about Q. He was simply explaining the ideas that the room had come up with. I urged him to explore the Maia Jordan relationship without plot, much like we did with the flashbacks between Magnus and Alec in 218. Simply watching their relationship evolve and then crumble would be fine for me.

It was much warmer in Toronto this time, thank God. We arrived at the studio to find it had been beautifully remodeled with new signage everywhere. We toured the new sets with Matt and Doug, my eyes wide and my jaw on the floor. Doug and his team outdid themselves, as anyone who has seen season three can attest to. I couldn't lavish enough praise on Doug and his team. On any show, but particularly a sci-fi/fantasy show, production design can either make your material soar or deflate it in the goofiest of ways. Doug and his team elevated the look of the show in ways I could only dream of.

Between production meetings and the table read, we did our round of cast meetings. Isaiah brought a bundle of firewood, jokingly commenting that it was appropriate for our fireside chat. Emeraude had just come from a facial, beautiful and elegant as always. Dom had just flown in from England. Kat was eager and excited about discovering her new dual blades and the action scenes she was about to embark on. Matt told us about being recognized more and more lately and believed the ratings were going to increase as more people discovered the show. Harry described his recent cross-country drive from L.A. to Toronto. Alberto was passionate about a new documentary he was producing with his talented younger brother. Alisha was thrilled about being a series regular and intrigued by the upcoming storyline with Jordan Kyle. The entire cast felt more comfortable with us.

The cast dinner was intimate, relaxing, and an opportunity for us all to celebrate the chance to make twenty more episodes. Harry was sweet enough to FaceTime with my Glee-obsessed daughter for a few minutes, which made her entire year. Matt Daddario displayed his encyclopedic knowledge about jewelry of all things. As I quickly learned, Matt was exceptionally bright and knew much about many different things. I sat next to Kat, who felt like she was literally growing up before my very eyes. It had been a year since we began on the show, and the girl who we met that first time in Toronto was now a mature young actress coming into her own. It was a joy to witness. Fun was had by all, and the next morning we flew back to L.A. to tackle the rest of season 3a. We would see them all soon in New York for yet another Comic-Con.

# SALT IN THE WOUND

With production beginning in Toronto, my life became busier as Darren and I now had to juggle production meetings, editing, mixing and coloring along with managing the writer's room and, of course, actually writing. We still made time for our wine and cheese viewing parties with staff every Monday evening at 5pm sharp, but that would conclude soon with the season 2b finale. The staff appeared to be bonding in a big way, which of course made me happy, but also left me feeling a bit alienated. I was on the outside looking in at their inside jokes and cozy rapport, treated more like a boss than a colleague, which of course I completely understood. I was also twenty-five years older than most of them, and subsequently had different tastes and references. We were from and living in two different worlds, and while I sometimes felt that distance and separation, more often I felt a bond as we came together to create stories for the shadow world.

307 aka "Salt in the Wound" proved to be one of the most difficult episodes to break. My desire to simplify the Maia/Jordan flashback story was met with cool indifference by the writers, so much so that I had to share my frustration and explain that after doing twenty-six episodes of the show, the staff simply had

to trust us. Eventually people came on board, but it wasn't easy. The show would provide the introduction of another book character, Jia Penhallow, played with stern conviction by the wonderful Francoise Yip, while saying goodbye to Imogen in the most tragic way possible. In the initial pitch to the network, the search and retrieval for Jace was much more complex and plot heavy. I was wary when I was first pitched the story by the room, but after battling for the Maia/Jordan story, I was reluctant to put up more resistance, increasing the friction with the staff. When they heard the pitch, The Powers That Be felt it was difficult to follow and urged us to regroup and come up with another story, which we all did.

Celeste Vasquez, writing her first ever solo TV script, did a fantastic job, and her ability to write scenes which contain multiple characters was outstanding. Those scenes were the toughest and least enjoyable to write, act and direct, but they were a necessary part of the show at times, especially during a crisis when everyone is learning at the same time that Jace is the Owl. The exchange between Maia and Jordan about how to say plural octopus, with Maia's "I'm pretty sure it's octopuses. Look it up" is pure Celeste - wry and sarcastic with a bite at the end.

Joshua Butler returned and directed what I believe is his best episode of the show. The look, performances and pacing are spot on, and he deftly handled the change of tone from scene to scene. Jace killing Imogen is perhaps one of the most violent, disturbing scenes of the entire series. Again, the locations were staggering in scope, especially the beach. Folks VFX had to add little waves in the background because it's actually a lake, not an ocean. Maia and Jordan's first "I love you" and their gentle kiss in his car is romantic without being cheesy, a stark contrast to Jordan's wolfing out in that same car later and ending up curled up naked on the ground, Maia's blood on his hands.

308 aka "A Heart of Darkness" was an opportunity to spend time with the real Jace and see and feel his pain and overwhelming guilt over his recent murderous behavior. Darren and I had done several "journey into character's mind" episodes in our career and always loved the conceit. Originally it was only Alec who was going to enter Jace's mind, but after the network's research team

paid us a visit to the writer's room and explained that viewers loved seeing the three Lightwood siblings together, I suggested we bring Isabelle along for the journey as well. It proved to be a smart suggestion because it inspired Jamie Gorenberg to come up with one of my favorite lines of the entire series - "three go in, three come out" - a line that brings me to tears every time I watch it. It was also a chance to bring back the younger versions of themselves, although we had to recast young Izzy when the actress from 203 came in to audition and was now almost a foot taller than the boys.

The Clary story was difficult now that she was in captivity. We knew how it was going to end, with Clary being sentenced to death, but her trial seemed anticlimactic since the viewer knew everything that would be discovered by Jia. Using the soul sword was a nice throwback. Seeing Jia in all her evil glory was a cool way to set her up as a hardliner. Kat's performance was strong as always, but in the end, it ranks as one of my least favorite subplots we've done, and I can only blame my stubborn self. Thankfully the journey into Jace's mind was so powerful and moving that it ended up becoming the real identity of the episode, one of the most emotional ones of the series.

When Mary Viola first brought up the idea of Ari Sandel directing an episode of Shadowhunters, Darren and I immediately recognized the name with great fondness. Way back on MELROSE PLACE, Ari had directed a series of webisodes for us that would air before the launch of the show. They starred Max Greenfield, who would go on to have great success on NEW GIRL, as a realtor trying to sell apartments in the infamous apartment complex. Ari had won an Academy Award for his short film, WEST BANK STORY, and was clearly talented. He did a great job for us and went on to direct several features. We were surprised he wanted to direct a TV show, but when he came in for a meeting his passion was palpable. He even offered to shadow the director for 307 so he could be a fly on the wall and learn more about the show before he hit the floor. Darren and I were sold.

Jamie's script was terrific, but as I've learned over my many years writing television, a great script doesn't always translate into a great episode. In

175

the hands of a weak director, it can end up unwatchable. With the help of Production Designer Doug McCullough and David Herrington's imaginative cinematography, Ari managed to create a mesmerizing visual world inside Jace's head, as well as nurture performances that are some of the most powerful moments in the series. Dom was at the top of his game, his tears of pain seemingly real. Emeraude was particularly strong throughout the episode. Her scene with young Jace, when she sings the familiar song that proves her identity, is deeply emotional and heartbreaking. Emeraude was super nervous about singing on camera, but I assured her Izzy's voice should be far from pitch perfect. No one expected or assumed Isabelle Lightwood was Beyonce in hiding. Matt Daddario gave one of his most heartfelt performances outside of a Malec storyline, completely convincing as a hurting parabatai. I knew the fans were going to flip out.

# ANOTHER BITE AT THE APPLE

In early October on a Friday morning, Darren and I flew out to New York for yet another Comic-Con. This time we knew what to expect, and I was certainly more relaxed. I was also excited to see my oldest daughter Maya, who was in college at The George Washington University in Washington D.C. and was taking the train up to spend the weekend with me and spend a few days with her cousin in Brooklyn after I left. She had never been to a Comic-Con, and I knew she would be blown away. I also knew she'd be blown away by DEAR EVAN HANSEN, the play I had seen the year before with her sister when she was in Israel for her birthright trip (a free journey paid by the state of Israel for any Jewish American between the ages of 18 and 25). While Darren and I ate dinner at the hotel that night, she went to see the play, meeting me back in our room later as impressed as I was.

The next morning after breakfast, a hair and make-up person came up to the room and did their thing. As I said before, it was always awkward, even more so when your kid is watching. We went down in the lobby and met Darren and Matt Hastings, who was there with his wife and two adorable kids. We all hopped in a van that drove us to the venue, which was larger than the one from the previous year. Backstage in the green room, we met Kat, Alisha, Isaiah and Matt, who was there with his lovely fiancé Esther Kim. I had met Esther only briefly, and she could not have been nicer to my daughter. When we all went off to take the stage and then do press afterward, Esther took Maya under her wing and hung out with her for the duration. God bless her. My nephew-in-law Patrrick, the ultimate fan boy wearing his Malec T-shirt proudly, was there as well.

Before we hit the stage, we screened a trailer for season 3a full of moments from the first five episodes that had been shot. The cast had yet to see any footage and craned their necks to see the screen just like they did in San Diego. We were greeted on stage by a packed auditorium full of screaming fans carrying various signs. Our old friend Jim Halterman was the moderator, and the panel went smoothly. We announced the casting of Anna Hopkins and then played a pre-taped video from Javier Munoz, who couldn't be there in person due to his Hamilton commitment. The crowd went crazy. After the panel and a series of photos backstage with the cast and Karey Burke, we headed off to do our speed dial interviews. After now seeing the entirety of season 2, the press was warmer and more friendly than ever before. As I answered question after question, I saw my daughter from the corner of my eye watching with wide-eyed amazement. Both of my girls never really showed any interest in what I did for a living, besides raiding the craft services table when they visited sets as young children. But after seeing me on the panel and now in the press room, she was clearly impressed.

After the panel we jumped in a van to visit the mockup of the Jade Wolf that Freeform had built for the convention. Fans were everywhere and I got the opportunity to chat with several folks, all of whom had journeyed from far off places to attend the panel. It was inspiring to say the least. I took Maya to the convention floor so she could see and feel what a comic-con's really like, complete with the requisite body odor. It was all overwhelming for both of us. That night the two of us went for a sushi dinner and then to see WAITRESS, which we both thoroughly enjoyed. I had never been into musical theater until I had kids who joined a class at a community theater and performed everything from HAIRSPRAY to FIDDLER ON THE ROOF. When we got back to the hotel, we met the cast downstairs for a drink before retiring for the night. What a day.

I made sure to book my flight home late the following day so I would have a chance to spend as much time with Maya before heading back. We walked all over Manhattan, taking in the sights and sounds. At the end of the day I put her in a cab to take her to my niece's place in Brooklyn, happy tears in my eyes as the taxi pulled away into traffic. We had a magical time together. On the flight back to L.A. I was reading a script when the handsome young British fellow next to me politely asked if I was coming back from the Comic-Con. He introduced himself as Gregg Sulkin, one of the stars of Marvel's RUNAWAYS and one of the nicest guys you'll ever meet. My string of famous seatmates in first class continued.

# THE DUAL THREAT

The last two episodes of season 3a were the best consecutive shows we had yet to produce on the series. 309 aka "Familia Ante Omnia" and 310 aka "Erchomai" were essentially a two-parter and ended up airing that way on Freeform. They were each penned by writers who were both talented in the room and on the page. Taylor was young and inexperienced, Shadowhunters being her first TV writing job, but you'd never know it. Q of course was a seasoned pro with many episodes of television behind him. Together they delivered two hours of pure gold.

The story for 309 was as dense as they come, filled to the brim with golden moments and wonderful Easter eggs for book fans. Spending time inside the Gard provided not only tense drama but the opportunity for cinematic spectacle, a challenge that Matt Hastings relished. The return of Heidi in Simon's family dwelling created a kind of home invasion only possible in the shadow world. When Heidi manipulates Simon into feeding on his sister in front of his mother, the viewer would know there was no turning back for Simon now. He could never be normal again, no matter how hard he tried. Tessa Mossey was wonderfully terrifying as usual. Clary using a rune to bring back the dead came from the books, where she brought back a random dead shadowhunter. In the show, by bringing back her evil father, it made the act that much more personal and disturbing, with horrifying consequences. Throw in the epic warlock battle between Magnus and Lorenzo, and the episode was packed with memorable moments.

Taylor's writer's draft was fantastic. We had the fewest notes that we've ever had on a first draft, and most of what you see was there from the very beginning. I knew she was talented, but I had no idea how deftly she would handle such a complex story. Matt's direction throughout was masterful, every scene staggeringly good both emotionally and visually. The red robes of the prisoners against the grey palette of the prison was our own nod to THE HANDMAID'S TALE, the show that had recently premiered, written and developed by mutual friends of ours. The visual effects throughout were staggering. The musical score was epic. Truly there's not a frame of film that I have a problem with, a rarity in the process of putting any show together. I was awestruck when I saw his director's cut and felt the same way when I rewatched the complete episode years later.

310 was a sparser story with more time to let scenes breathe. We were all excited by Magnus' trek to Edom and the introduction of his father Asmodeus. The actor Jack Yang was a true find who could play both comedy and poignant drama with equal ease. We knew he would fit well in our canon and looked forward to using him more in season 3b. Becky accepting Simon for who he is was beautiful, the sibling bond theme that is seen so frequently with the Lightwood family just as powerful in the Lewis clan. Simon forced to encanto his Mom into believing he was dead shattered me on the page as well as on screen. The final Lilith face-off was everything we could have asked for and more. The only notes we had on Q's first draft was to "de-quip" it a bit so it wouldn't feel so humorous, but all the emotion was there from the beginning.

Jeff Hunt returned as director and shot the hell out of it, pun intended. Edom blew my mind, with much of the credit owed to Folks VFX, who created a world out of nothing. The blood-red sky filled with squawking wraith demons was

181

feature film level amazing. The teaser flashback with young Jonathan arriving in Edom to meet Lilith for the first time was originally going to be the teaser in 308, but it felt too shoe-horned in without enough context. The scene fit much better in 310. All the performances were strong, especially Alberto. The scene with his mom in the hospital chapel is perhaps some of his best work on the series, and the way he collapses into Izzy's arms afterwards brings me to tears every time. Holly Deveaux as Becky and Christina Cox as Simon's Mom also give their best performances of the series. We cast Conrad Coates, who we had worked with on DEFIANCE, as Luke's NYPD superior, and he crushed it just like he did on that show.

Darren and I travelled up to Toronto for the table read of 310. It was right before American Thanksgiving, and 309 was currently shooting. Taylor was on set for the first time, thrilled to be there. I felt bad that she wasn't able to be home with her family for Thanksgiving, until I saw that her family had come up to Toronto to spend the holiday with her. Meeting her Mom, sister, and niece, baby Stella, in the production offices moved me deeply. The table read for 310 went smoothly and our tone meeting with Jeff Hunt, with Q dialing in from L.A., made me feel thankful to be working with such talented people.

That evening Darren and I hosted a cocktail party at a local lounge for the cast, including those in supporting roles who we never got to spend time with. Our old friend Anna Hopkins was the first to show up, and it was wonderful catching up with her, just the three of us. Soon others begin to trickle in, including Kat, Dom, Alberto and Chai, who brought along a few of his dear friends from back home who were visiting. The warmth and sincerity that one sees in Chai on screen is truly a reflection of who he is behind the camera as well. Matt Daddario showed up but had to leave early to have dinner with his father who was visiting from out of town. It was touching to see that connection to his father. Nicola arrived soon after, as did Alexandra Ordolis, who had brought Ollie to life with such warmth and humor. I told her I was sorry to see her leave the show, but she understood her role had played itself out. Shelby, Harry's wife, appeared as well wearing her usual sweet smile. Harry and Javier were shooting their warlock battle that night, so neither of them could make it. It was a wonderful evening, full of lots of laughs and great conversation. They were truly a special cast.

# WILL THE REAL JONATHAN MORGENSTERN PLEASE STAND UP?

With Lilith banished back to Edom and Valentine officially dead and buried, the true-blue Jonathan would now be our big bad villain for season 3b. Even though Will Tudor wore the visage of Sebastian Verlac, he worked so well on the show that if he returned, we could explain his appearance the same way we did in 216, when Jonathan remarked that he simply liked Sebastian's looks better than his own. But sadly, Will Tudor was unable to return regularly in season three, so we began a new casting search for Jonathan, using the exact same audition scenes that we used a year ago.

Luke Baines' audition struck us immediately, not just because he was immensely talented in both a sinister and charming way, but also because he looked like he could actually be Clary's brother. He was Australian but you'd never know by his impeccable American accent. Luke had done a few independent films, but this would be his first television series, and we were thrilled that he would be a fresh face to viewers around the world. Everyone agreed and we hired him quickly. A week later Darren and I met him for lunch to fill him in on the details of his character. We arrived and sat at our table but there was no Luke. After twenty minutes we began to worry. What if he was a flaky actor who habitually showed up late? We had dealt with actors like this before and were mortified at the thought that we had just hired one. We went ahead and ordered, cursing our bad luck, when Luke casually strolled in, not in a hurry at all. When we nicely told him he was a half hour late, his face turned beet red, clearly shaken. His agent's assistant had given him the wrong time and he assumed he was right on time. We told him not to worry about it and offered him some of our sushi, but the awkward moment became a recurring joke between the three of us.

After we hired Luke, we discovered he was friends with both Dom and Kat through the cool young actor community in L.A. (Darren and I often wondered if there were any actors in L.A. that Kat and Dom weren't friends with). Because of that relationship, Luke had seen Shadowhunters before and was thrilled to be part of the cast, especially in such a vital role. Luke was clearly intelligent, a former corporate crisis P.R. consultant for a large telecom company in England and was interested in any and every detail we could share about this complex character. I left the lunch feeling blessed to have him in the shadow world. He was going to crush it.

In the book series it was Jace who was given the twinning rune that connected him to Jonathan, eventually changing his personality and bringing Jace to the dark side. But after spending ten episodes with Jace possessed by the Owl, we knew it would feel extremely repetitive if we followed that path. Hence the idea of Clary going dark and becoming seemingly irrevocably connected with her long-lost brother. We knew it was a major departure from the book that would upset many fans, but our storytelling sensibility told us it was the right thing to do. It also gave Kat the opportunity to play an entirely different side of Clary, something I knew she would relish.

Another departure from the book series involved the idea of heavenly fire being used by the Clave to change downworlders into mundanes. I loved the notion as soon as I heard it in the writer's room. It was especially relevant to living in America today under a government that looked down at anyone who was different than the norm. Isabelle would lead the charge that would uncover this conspiracy, giving her character more of a central role in the series plot than ever before. Emeraude never once complained about her role on the show, but we were aware that she had been sidelined too much and wanted to bring her to the forefront. We were also intent on finally beginning the march toward her endgame relationship with Simon. Emeraude and Alberto had electric chemistry between them, first felt in season one followed by every scene they shared together.

Magnus without powers was something we had talked about for a while, and we are all excited to finally be able to write it. It would test his relationship with Alec in ways that had never been explored before and provide Harry with an opportunity to play his character in a new and exciting way. Maia would finally mend her relationship with Jordan and become the Alpha she was always destined to be. Luke would end up not only losing his pack but his job on the police force as well, eventually forced to join the Praetor Lupus. More importantly and to the delight of many fans, he would finally begin a romantic relationship with Maryse.

In November, Darren and I and Claire made our pilgrimage to the network to pitch season 3b. The Powers That Be were excited by the deviations from the source material, realizing that if the show were to have real legs, we would need to create more stories that didn't rely on the books. Their one concern was that Clary might be gone from the Institute and our main cast for too long. We assured them it would only be two episodes - two episodes that we promised would be among the most memorable of the series.

311 aka "Lost Souls" and 312 aka "Original Sin" were conceived as a two-parter to be block shot by the same director, just as we had done with 219 and 220. Darren and I wrote 311 and Alex Schemmer wrote 312 before our Christmas break so that both scripts would be ready to go when production ramped up again in January. Originally the city of Kingston, Ontario was going to double for Paris, but Matt Hastings, the director of the block, pressed to shoot *in* Paris. Kingston was hours away from Toronto, so it would require a total company move that would cost almost as much as shooting in Paris with a French crew. Darren and I initially thought he was out of his mind, but he would not let it go. Like a dog

with a bone, Matt was tenacious in his conviction that the added production value from shooting in France was worth whatever the extra cost would be, even though it was only eleven pages of the script. Every great director I've ever worked with had that bulldog tenacity, and Matt was no different. After much back and forth discussion with the network, they finally agreed. We would shoot the Paris scenes at the end of the production schedule after the Toronto crew had wrapped. The interior scenes in Mirek's shop were shot on our stages, with visual effect plates of the Paris street outside added in post-production. But the rest of the Paris content was all shot in France. God bless Monsieur Hastings.

The scope in both of the episodes was the largest we had ever done on the show. The vast plains of powder snow provided a production value we could only have dreamed of. When Folks VFX added in the mountains in the background, it was absolutely breathtaking. Jonathan and Clary were in Siberia. Folks also created the entire motel location out of nothing, when in reality it too was shot on our stages. Isaiah gives my favorite Luke performance in 311 as an obsessed father intent on finding his daughter, his string-laced investigative board pinned on the wall - an ode to A BEAUTIFUL MIND. Of course, the Paris locations speak for themselves. The new subway tunnel set, built specifically for 3b, felt real, especially when filled with water as it was in 311.

Luke Baines was even better than we anticipated. Jonathan's desire to be good felt so real and true. His love for his sister was both utterly creepy and incredibly pure. The manner in which Luke delivered his lines surprised me in the best way, adding layers of emotion and sympathy I never knew were there. The way he mutters "Earl Grey" under his breath after Clary dismissively sweeps past him makes my heart yearn for Jonathan in a way I didn't know was possible. I couldn't take my eyes off him when he was on screen, and he and Kat proved to be amazing scene partners, especially at the end of 311 when they learn how close they really are.

Magnus and Alec babysitting Madzie was something I had wanted to see for a while (along with Magnus and Alec dancing - more of that coming soon), and 311 provided the opportunity. They were the best Uncles a little girl could ever ask for, with Alec reading her Dr. Seuss stories and Magnus acting as the "stern" disciplinarian gently explaining it was time for bed. The night-light moment is hands-down one of my favorite scenes I've ever written on the show, and seeing the final crescent moon visual effect created by Folks made my heart melt. Of course, the sweet night had to be ruined by Iris Rouse, now on the lamb from the Clave, intent on getting her Madzie back.

Alex wrote a gem of a script for 312, even better than 303, which is saying a lot. The Malec training scene was staggeringly great on the page, Alec's "I didn't know you had a black belt in name-dropping" reminded me that this writer's talent knew no bounds. Matt Hastings and stunt coordinator Darren McGuire and his team choreographed it all like a magical, seductive dance, and my guess it has been rewatched more than a billion times my Malec fans across the globe. I knew seeing the two of them in bed just after having sex, still out of breath, helped to make up for our gaffe back in 207, and helped educate the ignorant that same-sex couples do indeed make passionate, heated love like the rest of us.

When I heard the pitch for Cain, as in *the* Cain from Cain and Abel, a daylighter vampire who had also been marked by the Seelie Queen and would help Simon on his journey to get it removed, I thought it was absolutely brilliant. Then Alex's sharp, smart dialogue and masterful scene work elevated the character in ways I didn't see coming. The wonderful actor Pasha Ebrahimi brought the role to life in the most dynamic of ways, terrifying and heartbreaking all at once, his eyes painfully haunted by guilt. As soon as we saw the dailies, we knew he'd be part of our canon as long as the show was on the air. In the series finale he was originally in the script for 321, helping Magnus in Edom, but Pasha was sadly unavailable.

The bookend of Jonathan in the apartment was both a poetic and frightening way to end 312. By now viewers knew that Jonathan's temper could have terrifying consequences, and his mad tantrum in his mother's apartment showed his torment in a most disturbing way. Jonathan would not go quietly into the sunset realizing he'd never be with his sister. He would come back savvier and more manipulative than ever.

313 aka "Beati Bellicosi" is sadly my least favorite episode I did on the show, and I have no one but myself to blame. Sure, there are wonderful moments, like Jace and Clary's first time and his romantic declaration of love straight from the pages of the book. Simon and Maia's break-up was beautiful. Romaine Waite as Griffin, the new head of the New York Clan, was a strong addition to the show. But the episode as a whole felt flat for me from the get-go. I knew the rune wasn't going to come off Clary, so the drama of that story never propelled me forward. But somehow I managed to convince myself through the process that it was all working. After seeing Mike Rohl's director's cut, we tried reshooting certain parts that didn't work upon our initial viewing, but it was like putting a band-aid on an infected wound. Again, I blame me and only me.

Luckily the episode that followed was a breath of fresh air that had me on the edge of my seat on every page and in every frame. After thirty-three episodes under our belt, we knew the episodes that played in the taut thriller genre worked well. FACE OFF, starring John Travolta and Nic Cage and coincidentally written by my sweet neighbor Michael Colleary, is one of my favorite movies and one of the reasons why I fell in love with the premise of the episode as soon as I heard it in the writer's room. Given some demons have the ability to shapeshift, it was the perfect attribute to give to Jonathan as a means for him to attempt to win Clary back into his favor. Coupled with Maia and Jordan locked in the Jade Wolf freezer and Magnus getting his magic back for a grave-robbing journey to Belgium with his boyfriend, the episode in its story stage had all the recipes for success.

Because it would be written over the holiday break, it would again be the freelance episode, this time written by the intrepid writer's assistant and our former assistant Zoe Broad. Zoe did a terrific job on her first television script and was backed up by Alex Schemmer, who took care of the rewriting duties while Zoe returned after the holiday to work her "day job" in the writer's room. Salli Richardson-Whitfield, the director of the classic 205, returned to helm the episode and did a marvelous job, combining the sweet romance of Jace and Clary's ice-skating date with the unnerving terror and suspense of Jonathan masquerading as Jace. The actors were all at the top of their game. It was a joy to see Javier Munoz back in action "exercising" in his home gym and sipping on his magical celery smoothie all while taunting poor Magnus.

I had assumed Kat knew how to ice skate because, well, she's Kat McNamara who can seemingly do anything and everything. As it turned out, she didn't know how to ice skate but was game to learn. Matt Hasting's amazing assistant Kaylie Witcher, a talented ice skater herself, took Kat out and gave her a few pointers before filming, and on camera Kat did a fantastic job. Of course, a stunt skater helped out at times but what you see is pretty much Kat all the way. That sequence remains one of the most beautifully romantic scenes ever done on the show.

My only real beef with the episode is the use of the same location twice in the episode, under a row of archways at the University of Toronto. First during the day when Clary tells "Jace" about the carving on her arm and then at night when Isabelle and her team arrive to take Jonathan down, but Clary is unable to draw the somnambulus rune. Oh well. Hopefully not too many people noticed, but these things can drive a showrunner bonkers. In the end it's a particularly strong episode and a wonderful television debut for Zoe.

# MERRY XMAS

Before I knew it, the holiday break was upon us, but unlike the previous year, when I was wracked with anxiety about how well the premiere would do and how the world would receive the new look and feel of Shadowhunters season 2, I was totally relaxed and looking forward to spending a holiday away from the shadow world. I excitedly bought gifts for every member of the staff from me and Darren based on how I perceived their interests: A North Carolina basketball book for Brian; a Rick and Morty t-shirt for Taylor; a book on women's soccer for Celeste; a Dr. Who cookbook for Claire; a scuba diving book for Jamie; a used Making of "Raiders of the Lost Ark" paperback from the eighties, and the list goes on. Sweet Kat gifted Darren and I with beautiful matching beautiful parabatai leather coasters and keychains, one of the most thoughtful gifts I've ever received. It was a Christmas to remember.

The morning after our last day I jetted off to Hawaii with my wife and two daughters to spend a week of quiet relaxation in tropical paradise. Marc Kahn, our post producer/party planner/travel agent recommended Oahu, an island I had never been to, and it was just as glorious as he described. I spent much of the trip reading the biography of Alexander Hamilton by Ron Chernow in anticipation of seeing the play in Los Angeles when I returned. My voracious reading habits as a child continued into adulthood, and when not working, I preferred to read rather than watch TV with the exception of my beloved Lakers and Dodgers and news programs. In all the writer's rooms I've been in, there is always much bonding over the latest episode of this or that, and I always feel like the outsider.

When we all returned and gathered in the writer's room, I made sure to stop down and hear from each and every one about their holiday break. I loved nothing more than to hear about everyone's adventures. As a writer on staff of a TV show, one often ended up sharing many personal stories and anecdotes in the writer's room. It instantly connected people who normally wouldn't be connected and created a found family atmosphere that was special. As a showrunner, writers were usually more anxious and on guard in your presence, so it was more difficult to get to know them on a personal level. But the first day of the room and the day after an extended break afforded me the chance to be my curious self without being too obnoxious. I went around the room hearing about their fun-filled adventures in New Zealand, Japan, Austin, Texas, Seattle, Colorado, Indonesia and other exotic locales. Eventually, it was time to tackle a new episode.

# TO THE NIGHT CHILDREN

Vampires have always intrigued me more than any other supernatural being. So the idea of devoting an episode toward their species felt overdue during our tenure and 315 aka "To The Night Children" would be our big swing. The show would be Heidi's swan song on the series, Raphael would return, Simon would "de-encanto" someone for the first time, and we would finally explore the great wonder that is Holy Water. Ethical decisions about laws and regulations would abound, giving it more of a political bend than the typical episode. That first day discussing the show we knew it would end with Magnus seizing on the floor of Alec's office, mumbling incoherently in Indonesian. 315 was going to be one hell of an episode.

As was his norm, Pete Binswanger delivered a strong script full of great dialog, Alec's "...and miss pancake day?" among the many gems. First assistant director Siluck Saysanasy was making his directorial debut, and the cast and crew were thrilled. A former child actor who began his career on "Degrassi", Siluck worked on season one as second assistant director and was promoted to first assistant director in season two. He was loved by all and everyone was extremely supportive and intent on helping make his directorial debut successful. Every director yearns for an environment like that, especially when it's your first time out, but Siluck was more than prepared based on his long experience behind the camera on many films and tv shows and, more importantly, his undeniable talent.

315 is both cinematically exciting and emotionally satisfying, full of powerful moments and strong performances. While the episode focused on the vampires, Maia was at the forefront seeking justice for her slaughtered pack, and Alisha delivers one of her best performances of the series. Maia's takedown of Heidi by injecting herself with Holy Water and then baiting the deluded vampire into biting her ranks as one of if not the most ingenious way to murder a bloodsucker. Heidi's greying decalcification and disintegration in the Dumort alley is another Folks VFX highlight, and Simon's disturbed reaction to her death is another Alberto gold star.

# COLD OUTSIDE, WARM INSIDE

While the writer's room continued on their creative roll, Darren and I flew out to Toronto for a few days for the 311 and 312 table read and our customary sit down with the cast. Toronto was a beautiful winter wonderland, blanketed with snow. Growing up and living in L.A., I am always in awe of snow, and this time was no different. And by now I had learned to dress appropriately with the proper gear, so the cold no longer bothered me. It inspired me.

The morning before the table read we met Luke Baines for breakfast at our favorite little diner near the hotel. He had both scripts in hand and was full of questions and ideas. I could immediately tell he was throwing himself into this role in a deep, profound way. Luke is a smart actor who approaches his work seriously. He knew the role of Jonathan Morganstern and the way we had written him was going to change his career on an international scale thanks to Netflix broadcasting the show in so many different countries. He wanted to be the best he could be, and the breakfast was proof of his dedication.

At the studio the cast and crew appeared totally relaxed after their long break and in a great mood, buoyed by the two strong scripts for 311 and 312 and the fan reaction at Comic-Con for the season 3a trailer. The questions about season four began to trickle in from both cast and crew, asking if we had heard anything definitive yet. We hadn't, but we told them based on the enthusiasm from the network and the growing worldwide fan base on Twitter, it was hard to imagine a scenario where the show would end after three seasons.

Many of the cast members were interested in directing. Isasaih had written a short film (a very good script I might add) and was planning on shooting it during hiatus. Harry, Alberto, Kat and Alisha were also interested in directing, and we encouraged them to sit in on any and all production meetings that they wanted to be in. Most directors welcome having a shadow who is there to learn from their experience, especially when it's an actor. Isaiah had shadowed a director on STITCHERS, and Alisha began showing up in meetings whenever she could, including the sound mix for 314 in L.A. where she suggested a great idea we ended up using about adding the buzzing of insects around the bloodied corpses in the The Jade Wolf.

The table read was exceptional for both episodes. Early on in season two, we had noticed a lot of the cast didn't take the table reads seriously. This can be a common problem on many shows, and we immediately nipped it in the bud after one too many lackadaisical efforts. The table read is a hugely important piece of the process because it allows us and the writers to make a last-minute tweak if the words aren't sounding right out of the actor's mouth. Once we sent a stern email to the cast educating them about our feelings, the actors immediately began to take it seriously, reading it and knowing the material beforehand so they could deliver a worthy performance. This table read did not disappoint, especially Kat and Luke, whose scenes felt like they were being performed on a stage.

After the table read Roger Chingirian introduced himself. Roger was the new cinematographer replacing David Herrington, a warm, soft-spoken man who had nothing but great things to say about the show and these upcoming two scripts. He was excited to start, and his enthusiastic newcomer energy inspired me. Matt had worked with him previously on THE ORIGINALS and was ecstatic when he was able to bring him into the shadow world. As soon as I saw the dailies for 311 and 312, I immediately knew why. Roger was a true artist who painted light and color in the most gorgeous of ways.

That night Chris Hatcher organized a lovely cast dinner in the backroom of a Toronto restaurant. Darren and I drove over with Chris, who filled us in on the latest backstage budget drama. I always had to pinch myself when I was reminded of how young he was. Chris had the smarts and savvy of a producer who had been doing this forever, and here he was having just turned thirty years old. We arrived to find Alisha and Emeraude. Matt Hastings soon appeared, and then the others swept in one by one, Harry the last to arrive due to a wardrobe fitting. The wine flowed and the food was plenty, the vibe warmer than it had ever been. The network and Constantin didn't make it out this time, so the dinner was truly the inner circle.

I stood up, clinked my glass, and suggested going around the room one by one and speaking about a memory they have of making the show. I knew it was kind of a cheesy thing to do but I also knew it would be fun - and I was totally curious. I went first to break the ice and spoke about the first time I saw the director's cut for 205 and realized Darren and I were going to be okay. Alberto talked about his first day on the pilot, and how nervous he was, standing there with the acclaimed director McG after graduating from NYU weeks ago. Harry spoke about the infamous goat baby in 205, where the prosthetic fell off the baby's feet and everyone was dying of laughter (when we got back to L.A., we found the deleted scene and asked Freeform to release it on Twitter). One by one they told their stories, mostly from season one when it was all brand new, and it was funny and emotional at the same time, much like an episode of Shadowhunters.

# THE DANCE

Since the first day of the season 3 writer's room, I had been pining for a Malec dancing scene that would make me and fans across the worldwide swoon with delight. My dreams were answered on that January afternoon when I first heard the teaser for 316 aka "Stay With Me" and practically fell out of my chair. I had never applauded louder in that writer's room and bowed down to them all. It was finally happening, and it was better than I ever pictured it.

The entire story break for the episode was one of, if not the strongest stories the writer's room had ever created. The Malec story would be at the heart of the episode, but early on we knew we didn't want to do a "will Magnus live or die?" show like we did with Max. The question would rather be, would Magnus ever willfully give up his magic or continue to risk his life? It was one of the most poignant Malec stories we had done on the show, and one that gave both actors many highly charged emotional scenes that we knew they would crush. Alec trying to get Lorenzo to remove Magnus' magic is one of Matt Daddario's best performances, soaring through a range of emotions before moving into his heartbreaking plea. Magnus in the infirmary explaining to Alec how empty he is without his magic is Harry at the top of his game. We knew we had done a very similar scene in 314, but this one felt different, Magnus more raw and vulnerable than we had ever seen him before, without his make-up, his hair flopped on his forehead. It broke my heart.

Lilith would also be at the center of the episode, elegantly woven between two stories - Jonathan's attempt to murder her in Edom and Clary and the Shadowhunters attempt to summon her from Edom. The stories would gracefully "kiss" when just as Jonathan was about to stab her, she's yanked back by the strength of Clary's summoning rune. One could call it coincidental, or totally awesome. I felt the latter when I heard it in the room. And I knew Anna Hopkins and Luke Baines were going to be squealing with glee playing that reunion scene between Mama and her beloved boy.

Jonathan and the Seelie Queen had a flirtatious then sexual relationship in the books and we were planning to do the same thing on the show, which meant unless we wanted to creep out ourselves and the audience in the ickiest of ways, it was time to say goodbye to the young Seelie Queen and morph her into a woman worthy of Jonathan's desire. Kimberly Sue-Murray had auditioned for episode 219 before Sarah Hyland came aboard, and we always had liked her audition. She auditioned again, as did Sydney Meyer, who expertly played the Queen at almost every table read. They were both fantastic. But at that point we knew Helen Blackthorn was about to make her debut in the following episode, and we instantly realized Sydney would be an awesome Helen. It would be a rare win-win situation for two great actors going out for the same role.

I knew Aisha would deliver a strong script, but her draft was superb. Our notes were tiny, and our pass was even tinier. For the first time in the history of the show, the Powers That Be had zero notes. Of course, production would dictate rewrites, but the people that were paying for the show believed the script was ready to go. This has almost never happened in our career, and it's a testament to not only Aisha and the writers that created the story, but to the executives at Freeform and Constantion who were secure enough in themselves to know when not to mess with something if you didn't need to.

Amanda Row returned to the greatness she displayed in 218, elevating an already great script into one of the best episodes of the series. She dove into the dance in a big way, emailing us a YouTube clip she had found from a wedding as a reference for how she saw the choreography. The competitive athlete in Matt Daddario (he's a great basketball player but hates dancing) knew if he was going to dance opposite Harry, he had to step up his game and make sure he knew his moves. And step up his game he did. But he wasn't the only one. Amanda's direction was masterful, delivering fanciful choreography, gorgeous cinematography, graceful editing, and incredible performances into a sequence that is its own beautiful short movie, complete with a beginning, middle and end.

The action sequences were all brilliantly done, mixing various film speeds like Amanda did so well in 218 during Jonathan's battle in the sub-cells. John Rakich found an abandoned electrical plant location that was apparently freezing cold. While the actors suffered, the location was spectacular. An action sequence with seven principal characters is an extremely difficult task to direct, but you'd never know watching the show. After watching her director's cut for 216, it was clear 218 wasn't just a rookie home run. Amanda Row was here to stay and have what will undoubtedly be a long, successful career.

# HEAVENLY FIRE

Episode 317 aka "Heavenly Fire" was an extraordinarily ambitious story for the show. Originally it was planned as a two-parter, the contamination of the water supply of New York forcing our Shadowhunters to deal with the downworld crisis. But it all felt too big to produce, as well as creating stakes that were simply too big for this stage in the season. Scaled down to fit into a single episode, 317 is wall to wall plot with a story that moves at lightning speed. It is one of the densest shows of the series, but luckily much of that density involves beautiful and emotional character moments that reveal surprising things about each of the people we've come to love.

Simon Lewis going undercover was a great anchor to the story, full of suspense, horror, pathos, and of course a little humor. Alberto loved the chance for Simon to go undercover and was intent on using an accent. Our initial reaction was that we felt an accent would distract the viewer and take them out of the show. We preferred Simon's normal voice because we thought it would be more relatable for the audience, and also funnier. But Alberto insisted on being able to audition a couple different accents for us. So we scheduled a call, and as I read

Helen in the scenes with Simon, Alberto performed Simon with a thick Bronx accent, a Cockney accent and a kind of prison psycho accent. They were all amazing. Alberto is an incredibly gifted actor, and I was thoroughly entertained. But after it was over we asked him to stick with good old Simon Lewis. The total pro, he went ahead and crushed the episode and never said another word about it.

We had wanted to bring back Victor Aldertree for quite some time and 317 was an ideal show for him to reappear. Nick Sagar is a wonderful actor and a human being, and I liked him in 201 even though I didn't understand why another character was being introduced into a cast of what felt like thousands. But his villainous manipulations turned out to be awesome throughout season 2a. It made sense that Aldertree was the bastard behind the Clave Conspiracy to make downworlders mundane, and it gave Izzy a chance to finally get revenge against the man who got her addicted to yin fen. Emeraude is terrific throughout the episode, especially in her scenes with Aldertree.

Celeste again was handed a story that was extremely complex and difficult to execute, but she managed it with great alacrity and skill. Her work was beyond that of a staff writer and after reading her first draft we knew we wanted to bring her back for season four. We gave Alex Schemmer the last Alec and Magnus scene to write because, well, we knew he could write that couple like no other, and the scene was such a monumental moment in their relationship, it felt right that he should carry that pen. The scene turned out to be absolutely gut-wrenching, both on the page and the screen.

Shannon Kohli was a camera operator on THE MAGICIANS who had recently made her directorial debut on that show. While she might have had a ton of experience directing before, she did an incredible job for us directing an epic episode. Her direction was just as ambitious as the script, and what she managed to pull off on the budget she was given was remarkable. We knew her camera work and shot-making would be strong, but we had no idea how deftly she would bring out so many wonderful performances. Sydney Meyer brought Helen Blackthorn to life in a way I was sure book lovers would appreciate as well as the fandom of the show. And her cross with Aline at the end was sure to make hearts swoon across the globe. The seelie ring conceit, which I worried would be ridiculous on camera, turned out to be way less cheesy than I imagined. One of my favorite scenes of the episode was the conversation between Simon, Raphael and dear old Iris Rouse debating the merits of being turned into a mundane against your will. All the flashbacks in Edom between Lilith and Jonathan felt as real and grounded as could be, and Luke Baines was exceptional as the young boy desperately looking for a way home.

# TRICK OR TREAT

Whenever we heard that Jenn Gerstenbatt was on the line, it was either really good news or something important enough was going on that she was involved. Initially we thought it was maybe an early season four renewal, but instead Jenn was calling to suggest we do a Halloween themed episode that would be broadcast near the holiday to help anchor Freeform's successful 31 Nights of Halloween, where they played a classic Halloween movie every night as well as their regular programming. Because new viewers often tuned in to see these movies, this could be a chance for them to sample Shadowhunters. I myself always thought holiday-themed episodes of TV shows were often lame and misguided, with stories that felt overly contrived and out of the wheelhouse of the show. We had been successful writing a Thanksgiving themed episode of SMALLVILLE called "Rage" and worked on the Christmas themed "Lexmas" the previous season, but beyond that had stayed away from the practice. But this idea felt like a good one in terms of attracting new viewers, as well as a creative challenge to create stories that would not only be accessible to someone who had never seen the show but would also continue the ongoing storylines. Sign us up.

At its core we knew it would be helpful if there was an outside character who could come into the shadow world and learn and discover all there is to know just as the new viewer would be doing the first time they watched. And what better character to do that than Becky Lewis, Simon's sister, who even though she recently learned he's a vampire she still wants to carry on the family trick or treating tradition. It was warm and sweet and provided the perfect place for exposition through the mouth of Simon, who would essentially be her tour guide through the shadow world. The other storylines would continue from the previous episodes, but would also be fairly self-contained, like Aec bringing back Asmodeus through the warlock shopkeeper. Or dark Clary eventually growing darker and freeing Jonathan.

Taylor Mallory, hot off 309 and her strong work in the writer's room, was a great choice to pen 318 being the true TMI fan on the staff. She did a solid job on the script that often felt like a throwback to season one. Josh Butler, who had already directed two episodes of the series, knew the series well by now and did a stand-up job managing the disparate tones throughout the show. There were many memorable moments, including the first Simon and Becky scene, the sweet Maia Jordan storyline, Jack Yang, and of course the Malec break-up scene at the end. Matt Daddario is outstanding in all of his scenes. But there are some moments that make me cringe. The hunt for the Devrak demons and the actual demons themselves aren't our shining moment. Any demon on two legs felt false, and the Devrak in particular felt wrong. Again, the only people to blame were Darren and I. We saw the preliminary designs and signed off, and when we saw the renderings in the cut, it was too late and too expensive to make wholesale changes. When it was over Darren and I promised to be more vigilant in the future.

# FAMILY OVER FILM

319 aka "Aku Cinta Kamu" was an episode I was particularly looking forward to because I was slated to direct. Directing was something I loved to do. In film school I always envisioned myself as a writer and director. I was blessed to be able to embark on a screenwriting career after college but directing became something I only dreamed of - until I found myself on Smallville working with Steve DeKnight, a writer from Buffy who came onto Smallville in season 5 with a deal to direct an episode each season. I could see that if I really wanted to do it I could make it part of my deal when I re-upped on the show, which I eventually did. Season seven episode ten provided my opportunity, and I dove into it with all I had. I was gifted with a fantastic story and script by Don Whitehead & Holly Henderson, a married couple writing team who we hired that season as staff writers and quickly proved to be incredibly talented. The directing experience was absolutely exhilarating, and the end result was appreciated by all. Because I was tapped to run the show the following season with Darren, Kelly and Brian, I suggested directing the second episode of my deal that season knowing my showrunner responsibilities would prevent me from disappearing to Canada for three weeks in season 8. The powers that be agreed, and I went off to direct the season seven finale, which included the emotional farewell for Michael

Rosenbaum aka the best Lex Luthor in Superman canon and one of the sweetest men you'll meet. On the night of his series wrap, between the jagged icicles in the Fortress of Solitude, Michael bought the entire crew what appeared to be hundreds of platters of sushi.

I had been advised not to write the first episodes that I would direct in order to concentrate solely on directing, which made sense to me. During season one of DEFIANCE as a consulting producer, I had the opportunity to direct a script that Darren and I wrote. It was an entirely different experience in that I didn't know any of the cast or crew like I did on Smallville. No one was rooting for me to succeed except for myself. It was a challenge that was both terrifying and incredibly satisfying once I proved to myself and everyone else that I indeed had what it took to direct a particularly strong episode of the series.

When I initially took on the showrunner job for Shadowhunters, I brought up the idea of directing. The network was okay with the concept but understandably wasn't comfortable with me disappearing for three weeks to Canada while trying to right the ship that was season two. They promised me I would direct in season three, and now here I was, pumped and ready to go.
The idea of doing another Magnus flashback story as he contemplates removing all of his memories of Alec was intriguing to me on an emotional and visual level. The opportunity to go to "Prague" and bring the beloved downworld club, The Bone Chandelier, to life excited me to no end. Maia and Jordan painting over the bloodstains in the Jade Wolf, their intimate moment interrupted by Raphael with news that he's been turned into a mundane was a powerful moment that would launch their hunt for the serum that could return them to a normal life. As I expected, Jamie G wrote a great script and I was psyched to bring it to life.

A week before I was set to fly to Toronto, my wife took my daughter to the east coast to look at a few colleges during her spring break. While in Boston, her leg began to swell, and she became so ill she had to be hospitalized. It was enormously frustrating being away from her, as the doctors took test after test struggling to find the cause of her dangerous symptoms. They finally released her without knowing the cause, and she and my daughter returned the night before I was to leave. I was hesitant to leave her, but she assured me she'd be okay. She knew I had been looking forward to directing for a long time.

On the flight to Toronto a pit in my stomach began to form. I had been away from my wife and family for much longer than three weeks but never when they were sick and under duress. It simply didn't feel right. The pit continued to grow, and I spent a sleepless night weighing my options. Siluck Sayanasy, who was scheduled to be my first AD, just directed 315 and was more than capable of replacing me. We would simply have to find another 1st AD, which wouldn't be that difficult. I could stay a few days to help guide the prep and then fly home to be with my wife. Or I could soldier on and direct the episode, communicating with my wife via phone and FaceTime to lend her my support. It didn't take me long to make my decision. As soon as I got to the studio in the morning, I told Chris, Hastings and Siluck my plan. They were all incredibly supportive, as were the Powers that Be after they saw the cut of 315. As we all hopped in a van to go location scouting and find our Bone Chandelier, I was immensely relieved, as was my wife. I would be home in a few short days, and Siluck would end up directing another strong episode, featuring one of my favorite scenes of the series: Madzie asking Alec and Magnus for permission to warlock-magic sprinkles on her ice cream cone, and their differing parenting styles. A pure Malec moment if there ever was one. And my wife turned out to be a-okay. Everyone won.

# THE EVE OF SEASON THREE

With only one episode left to break in the long season, the writers were excited about their upcoming break and already planning their vacations. Season four felt fait accompli at this point, and we assumed we would all be back again after Memorial Day weekend. The only question was how many episodes the order would be. We had heard rumors of fourteen, sixteen, you name it. But the future looked bright. Q was in full command of 320, an episode he would be penning, and the story-break, like his writing, happened at lightning speed. The plan from the beginning was to end the episode and season with Isabelle burning with heavenly fire after her sweet kiss with Simon. It was a huge break from the book story, where Clary was the one infected, but we knew Clary's infection would feel redundant after her possession story in 3b. Also, Izzy was also the one who first led the investigation into the heavenly fire conspiracy in 313, and the twist would be a cool climax to that story. It would also be a wonderful way to inject yet another barrier between her and Simon in season 4.

A vulnerable Magnus slipping into his father's warm embrace was a moving storyline and a wonderful showcase for the electric chemistry between

Harry and Jack Yang. Their father son dynamic was deliciously weird yet relatable. The way they reduced Lorenzo Rey to a lizard together had me cheering from my seat. The Clary-Jonathan story came to a tragic end with Jonathan gaining his wings and soaring off into the sky in a tormented rage. Luke Baines was amazing. Dark Clary felt strangely believable thanks to Kat's incredible performance, and her guilt in the aftermath was heartbreaking. Matt Hastings directed another breathtaking episode, but it was significantly over 42 minutes, so tough cuts would have to be made.

Once the production of 320 wrapped in Toronto in early April, Matt Hastings led the charge to Paris to film the scenes for 312, a scene in 319 that would double as Prague, and a few scenes in 320 that would double as downtown Alicante. Kat, Dom and Luke would be the only cast members to make the trip, along with a few key crew members. Darren and I were tempted to go but knew there wasn't much we could add to the filmmaking process on the ground, and as fiscally prudent showrunners, we thought it would be a waste of money. Save it for season four, right?

In mid-May, we had our season three wrap party the evening that 309 and 310 aired together, as well as the day of the Freeform Upfronts in New York. Harry and Isaiah had been invited and were attending, and we all assumed that the show's pick-up would be announced then. At five pm a few of the writers gathered with us in our editing bay to watch and live-tweet the shows over wine and cheese. But still no news about the pick-up. Afterwards we walked to a nearby restaurant to celebrate the season. Weeks ago I imagined it would also be a celebration of the pick-up, but instead it was like listening to one long continuous "have you heard anything yet?" all night long, and then speculating why we hadn't.

# THE CALL THAT CHANGED IT ALL

I was in the editing bay working with Karen and Marc on the finishing touches for 319 when my cell phone rang. It was Jenn Gerstenblatt, Brian Lenard and Kirsten Creamer calling from the network for me and Darren. Darren was on holiday up in Big Sur for Memorial Day weekend and instructed me to take the call if it came in. This was the call. Karen and Marc knew something was up as I quickly stepped out of the editing bay.

Jenn's voice came on the line, cheery as usual as she explained she had good news and bad news. The bad news was that Netflix was cancelling the show. The good news is that they've agreed to do two more episodes to wrap up the series. For a quick moment I thought it was some bizarre cruel joke, but I soon realized this was really happening, as they went on to explain we would have part of our writing staff back to help with those episodes and they would try to give us a bigger budget to produce them. I was absolutely speechless, which is very rare for me. I had thought the show was hugely popular for Netflix due to the worldwide fandom, but I guess I was wrong. She made me promise to only share the news with Darren because they were still in the process of figuring out how to break the news to everyone else. I slowly nodded, overwhelmed by the poetic circularity of my involvement in the shadow world. What began by a discreet phone call from Jenn Gertsenblatt that came totally out of blue ended the exact same way. I told them I had to tell the writers. Their lives had been on hold and we owed it to them. Besides, the writers who were contracted to come back were expected to begin in a matter of days. They completely understood. I hung up, numb, pondering whether to call Darren now and ruin his holiday weekend. Would I want to be interrupted by this horrendous news? I decided it wasn't really my choice to make. If I knew the news, he should too.

The slew of painful phone calls announcing the news to all the incredibly creative, talented artists who had put their hearts and souls into the show was the worst part about my entire time in the shadow world. Call after call, I listened to the disbelief and heartbreak in their voices and went about trying to explain our misfortune. The good news really was good news. Being able to create two hours of television that would wrap up the series was an awesome, creative challenge that I actually looked forward to. I had never been able to say goodbye during a series finale because I was always hoping for another season. In this case, there was an end we all see coming and the way we reach that end will be a very special journey, filled with unforgettable moments that will both satisfy you and make you want more.

The following week the writers dutifully showed up at our depressing offices in the bowels of Hollywood to try and concoct two more hours. We were only allowed to bring back the upper level writers, which of course included Q, Jamie, Brian Milikin and Pete. All of us were in a state of disbelief and depression, but we knew we had to not only get through it but create something special. Q arrived with all guns blazing, full of ideas, most of which you see on screen in the final episodes. He took charge as he had been doing since 301 and bonded us and the material together in a wonderful way. We quickly found out that Isaiah and Alisha would each only be available for a few days for the shoot. Isaiah scored a major role in the movie IT CHAPTER TWO, and Alisha just booked the lead for RAISING DION. I was thrilled for both of them. We would simply have to write around it, and that we did.

That first day back, late in the afternoon, the cancellation was announced in the press and everything changed. My depression was quickly lifted as the outpouring of shock and disbelief poured in from all over the world. I knew fans were not going to be happy, but I didn't realize how many people were genuinely upset, some even devastated, and how inspiring the collectiveness of their grief was. While writing the script for 322, Darren and I were called out of our office by Claire who was pointing up at the sky, at an airplane flying a "Save Shadowhunters" banner over the Netflix building a mile east of us. I was awestruck, and more inspired than ever to deliver a finale that would satisfy and inspire them.

It was a no-brainer that Matt Hastings would direct the finale, but we didn't know what crew would stay and what crew would go on to other jobs. They had all been counting on at least fourteen more episodes, and now they were left with only two. We of course completely understood. When the call came in later in the week from Matt Hastings explaining he was just offered another job that would sadly start right away and prevent him from directing the two-parter, we were stunned, but again understood. We thought about which director would be best to replace him and who was actually available in three short weeks. Two names came to mind. Jeff Hunt had directed 217 and 310 and was a seasoned pro capable of tackling something as massive as this would be. Amanda Row was a superstar on the rise who shot 218, 303 and 316, and while not having a vast amount of experience, it was clear she understood the show on a deep level.

And then I thought about me. After stepping away from 319, I assumed I would direct in season four, but that wasn't going to happen. It was the series finale or nothing. Before I brought it up to anyone, I deliberated with myself, wondering if I wanted to take on such a huge responsibility and leave my family for seven weeks. And if I did, was directing a selfish act or something that was best for the show? I knew I was a good director, but I had nowhere near the experience I, as a showrunner, would want in the person at the helm of the two-hour series finale. On the other hand, no one knew the show like I did. Darren and I had pored over every word and every frame of the last forty episodes on computers, in editing bays and on mixing stages. I had seen what worked and what didn't work on every director's cut, and I knew I could deliver something special. Before I got my hopes up too high, I knew I needed Darren's support if this crazy plan of mine had any chance of becoming a reality. He didn't even blink. He was totally behind it. I spoke with Matt Hastings, who was also supportive, and before I knew it, on a summer morning in late June, I was flying up to Toronto for seven weeks to prep and shoot the finale.

# SEVEN WEEKS OF SUMMER

The solitude and insomnia during those first two weeks of prep was overpowering. I had never spent more time in my own head in my entire life. Luckily the network was kind enough to put me up at a mind-blowing luxury hotel called the Shangri-La, where I spent endless hours storyboarding every shot and going over every detail and moment in the two scripts while listening to my homemade Shadowhunters playlist on Spotify. On Sundays I allowed myself to sneak out for a matinee to clear my head, one of them being BLOCKERS, which had the catchiest tune ever over its closing credits, Lizzo's "Good as Hell." I couldn't leave the theater. When I got back to the hotel, I quickly emailed Lindsay Wolfington asking if we could use that during the dance at the Malec wedding. It ended up being too expensive, but I did play it on set between takes so Anna and Harry could finally have their much talked about "dance off." It was an amazing moment that Mike McMurray ended up filming off the monitors on his phone.

One of the reasons I was so excited to direct was the chance to get to know the talented crew and truly see how the show was made on a daily basis. As a showrunner in L.A., I only knew these folks at an arm's distance, on the phone or on a Skype call during a production meeting, but never one on one. During my sixteen days of prep I got to spend time with each and every one of the department heads and witness their incredible creativity and artistry from a front row seat. It was enlightening and heartening, and I cherished every minute. They were all invested in the show and wanted this finale to be just as spectacular as I did. As a director you are continually presented with choices by these talented people - sets, props, costumes, prosthetics, hair and make-up ideas, paint colors, you name it. I marveled at the brilliance of these talented people and felt blessed I was part of something that felt so special.

Darren flew out to Toronto for the table-read and the 312 sound mix. It was great to see him and have him be part of the wondrous journey. Matt Hastings, who was now on another show in Vancouver, also flew in for the two events. The 312 mix, with the Paris footage now expertly edited into the final cut, was a moving experience, our last mix with the three of us together. Matt's young boy was there as well, a beautiful precocious kid with long, golden locks who seemed to move through life with a graceful ease. Technicolor served us champagne for the occasion - none for the little one of course - and Paris never looked or sounded better.

The table-read was a somber affair. It was the first time I had seen most of the cast since the show had been cancelled, and everyone appeared totally shell-shocked. Before it began, I ushered everyone into Chris Hatcher's office and spoke from my heart. We were about to embark on these last two episodes, a farewell to the fans, and I wanted the experience to be as special and memorable as possible. I was aware that they had all perceived me as their boss up to now, but for these last two shows I would be their creative partner on the floor, hopefully coaxing the best performances from all of them. Their faces were so raw and vulnerable. I could see the pain and confusion in their eyes realizing that this show that they had spent the last four years of their young life working was coming to a crashing conclusion. As someone quite older who's worked on many different shows, I promised them that Shadowhunters was a unique experience that they will always remember. Many actors work their whole careers without experiencing a fanbase as passionate and special as this one. Harry, who also worked on Glee, was fortunate to have worked on two shows like that, but I explained how rare that was. While the show was ending, we should all feel blessed to have been a part of it.

As he normally did, Matt Hastings read the scene description during the table read. All the actors gave it their all, especially Kat, who fought back tears as Clary's memory slowly faded away. Her tears affected all of us, no more so than Matt, whose own emotions prevented him from reading. He nodded to me to continue. I could barely hold it together as I stammered through the last ten minutes, tears flowing down my cheeks. When it was over, we all hugged and shook hands, and then took a few pictures for the network social media people, who were on hand to document the entire finale experience. Besides Sydney Meyer, there was another table read actor who was also superb in every scene he read. Farid Yazdani had been there since season two, and we wanted to find a role for him as well. In 321 it was originally Raj who was kidnapped from Wrangel Island by the Seelie Queen only to get incinerated by Jonathan. When the actor Raymond Black was unavailable, I suggested Farid get the role, and he ended up being absolutely awesome.

My first day of directing was in Magnus' apartment with Harry and Matt, when Magnus presents a wedding invitation to Alec and suggests they get married that evening. As the shooting crew gathered on set for the eight AM call, I realized I barely knew these talented people who came to work every day for fourteen hours plus to help lend their talents to bringing these scripts to life. This community was the blood of the show, the life force, and I was basically a stranger. When Matt and Harry arrived to block the scene, I was seized upon a desire to make a speech, to let them know how much I appreciated their tireless work that led to the show's success. I also needed to apologize for the cancellation. Even though I knew it wasn't my fault, I couldn't help but feel like I let all these people down.

Once I started the day was pure joy. Matt and Harry were incredibly collaborative and open to my ideas. At one point Javier Munoz swept in, as charming as ever for his portrayal of Lorenzo Rey. He was excellent, take after take. The man was locked in. They all were. Plates of wedding cakes suddenly appeared, Harry's eyes lighting up as he examined the various frosty delights. In the evening we shot the last scene, in the City of Glass with the High Warlock of Alicante and his Consul husband. Matt and Harry recognized a martini moment that they could rhyme with a moment from season one, and I thought it was great. Before the last take, I reminded them that this would be the last time they'd be in Magnus' apartment. This was the last scene. It was an emotional moment for all of us.

Alisha flew in from the set of RAISING DION in Atlanta for one day to film her scenes in 321 and 322. She was totally prepared and nailed first take after first take in all of her scenes. I was blown away. It was clearly an emotional day for her, the last time she'd be in the Jade Wolf. The last time she'd be in the Shadow World. She was extremely grateful that we were able to accommodate her schedule so she could do this new show. Originally Maia was part of the trek to Edom in "Alliance," but we had no problem rejiggering her story in order for Alisha to pursue this wonderful new opportunity. She still got a few juicy scenes to play and she was great in every one of them.

Isaiah came in on a Sunday for his work in the Praetor mansion with Praetor Scott and his work in the Institute with Clary. He too was appreciative for allowing him to go and film IT CHAPTER TWO during the finale. I told him it was the least we could do. This role was a huge opportunity for Isaiah, and I couldn't have been more excited for him. My wife and daughter Cami came to the set that day, and Isaiah was incredibly sweet. They were on yet another college trip to see Cornell and came to Toronto to visit for a few days. It was great to spend time with them on my day off, and then have them see me on set. Cameron had never seen me direct, and I could tell she was impressed even though she'd never, ever, tell me that. Isaiah finished his work that day, but I had one more scene to shoot. It was Kat and Emeraude's parabatai scene. At the end of the scene Isaiah showed up with trays of champagne for the cast and crew to toast his series wrap.

Much of the premiere was shot during a six-day week to accommodate the various conflicting schedules of such a large guest cast. On a Saturday off, as was now my custom, I went to see a matinee. EIGHTH GRADE was a fantastic movie. I was riveted from the first frame. It was a nice reprieve from my racing thoughts about directing in the shadow world, and I enjoyed every minute. It ended at six pm, and I was headed back to my hotel to change and get ready for dinner with Philippe and Pierre Henry, the excellent first AD on the even episodes in season 3b, when I saw Alberto and the stunt coordinator Darren Mcguire together in an outdoor bar. They waved me over, where I soon saw Dom, Kat, Luke, Darren's wife and a few other of their friends having drinks. Before I knew it Matt Dadarrio was there with his now wife Esther. Jade Hassoune appeared. Emeraude showed up with Ms. Make-up Master Amanda O'Leary, followed by Anna Hopkins, then Kimberly Sue Murray. The party was growing exponentially, and I quickly phoned Philippe to cancel dinner and have him join us here.

My walk to the hotel had turned into a joyous celebration. I didn't feel like anyone's boss. I felt like one of the shadow world gang. I showed Anna Hopkins the dance off video Mike McMurray took on set between her and Harry. She told me to put it on Twitter, but I was reluctant. Would it spoil the scene from 321? Anna was relentless, and before I knew it I hit send, a fortunate event for the fandom who got to enjoy those forty seconds of Anna and Harry on the Edom dance floor. Emeraude and Luke got me to FaceTime Darren. It was a night to be remembered, full of joy and laughter. I was shooting tomorrow with Luke and Kat - the giant sequence of Jonathan on his violent march through downtown Toronto toward the Institute and Clary's last-ditch attempt to stop him once and for all. Sunday was the only day we could close off the busy street, so I ducked out early from a celebration that would inevitably carry into Sunday.

I walked to the location that Sunday morning, as it was only six blocks from the hotel in the heart of downtown. It was a strange feeling to arrive with a cup of Starbucks to see the streets eerily empty with the exception of the crew. Weeks earlier I led the crew on the tech scout where I explained how I was going to shoot each scene and what would be required on the day. But that was during the week when it was bustling with pedestrians and cars. Today it was quiet. The call time was at noon, which meant I only had seven hours to shoot the three scenes before the light would be lost. I knew I had to move fast, but when you're working with drones and doing stunts, however small they might be, time tends to tick away at a rapid rate. At six we had to stop for dinner knowing we had to finish Clary smothering Jonathan with her VFX wings. Knowing time was of the essence, I had dinner in a restaurant literally adjacent to the set with Philippe, Chris Hatcher and Melissa Girotti, the amazing unit production manager and sweet soul who was nice enough to procure me amazing Blue Jays tickets during my lonely days of prep.

As soon as dinner was over, we quickly assembled around Kat and Luke, who instantly picked up where they left off, Clary holding her brother in a dying embrace. As the sun rapidly set, I quickly guided the incredible steadicam operator Michael X, who circled the two actors as Jonathan crumbled to the ground. With darkness falling, I knew we would have to adjust the lighting later in color-timing. I was more focused on the performances, which were both staggeringly good. Once we finished the scene, we all walked a block to where we would be filming the last scene of the finale, outside in the narrow walkway when Clary chases after Jace and recognizes his rune. Kat and Nancy Warren, the head of the hair department, had auditioned a wig for me earlier in the shoot that would help differentiate Clary's look from her shadowhunter look. Kat looked amazing in the wig but I worried it was too different. I sent a pic to Darren who liked it, so we went ahead and made the decision to use it. That night looking at the monitor, her hair looked magnificent, even though the wind from the drone carrying camera that rose above her during the last shot of the finale looked like it was going to blow the wig right off.

The night before the wedding ceremony I barely slept a wink. Of all the scenes I was shooting, the Malec wedding was something I knew would be a deeply profound experience for many, many people around the world... unless I fucked it up. I knew it had to be perfect. There wasn't a single decision that I didn't agonize over. I spent countless hours thinking and rethinking and designing the seating chart. Who was sitting with who meant a lot. And who was in that audience said a lot about Magnus and Alec, so I spent extra time choosing the extras and weighing in on their wardrobe and make-up to make it feel just right, and then of course sitting them in the right seat so it would make sense (shadowhunters on one side, downworlders on the other) as well as look cool. I chose one tuxedo for Magnus and then changed my mind at the last minute to replace it with what you see onscreen. I received sage advice back in the day from Miles Millar, my former boss on Smallville, who told me never to be afraid to change my mind if something doesn't feel right. Always trust your instinct.

Almost every principal character who had ever been on the series was there for the ceremony, all dressed to the nines, which meant the day was a wonderful reunion for much of the cast. Young Jack Fulton, who played Max, the youngest of the Lightwoods, was grinning from ear to ear the whole day, relishing the opportunity to hang out again with his Lightwood family. None of them had any dialogue today except for Harry and Matt, but they were all excited and deeply invested in the shoot. Wardrobe and hair and make-up hired many more personnel to deal with the huge number of cast members who all had to look fabulous. I had ten hours to shoot the ceremony and I used my time wisely thanks to a meticulous shooting plan I had drawn up weeks before. With Ruelle's "I Get to Love You" blasting over speakers, I acted as the MC, signaling each of the wedding party when to begin their march down the aisle and the audience when to stand and sit. Like many weddings I've attended in the past, our little flower girl was getting cold feet. Ariana Williams was a great actor, but she was used to acting with a small group of actors and crew. Now she was required to walk down the aisle waving her hands in front of a hundred people, and she was clearly a little unnerved. I'm a kid's person and tried to talk to her but she was having none of it. The one person who was able to get through to her? Matt Daddario.

In order to manage my time and the cost of all the extras, I shot the audience and their reactions first before turning around and facing the stage, where we would shoot the vows only with Harry, Matt, Dom and Sophia. As they recited the words that Darren had so beautifully written, Harry and Matt were standing before an empty set but you'd never know watching the show. They were both totally locked in. They knew and felt how important this moment was, and both of their performances are living proof. When it was over, I embraced both of them and told them how special they were. Their performance that day was going to touch so many people.

The shooting days quickly became a blur of pure joy, sweat and tears. Each morning at call I made an appreciation speech signaling out a particular department and thanking them for all their hard work. It usually ate up two to three minutes of the day and it was worth every second. These skilled on-set crew members too often remain in the shadows and I wanted to shine the light on each and every one of them. Appreciation Monday for the greens department took place on the balcony of the L.A. Institute between the palm trees. Appreciation Wednesday for the AD's (Assistant Directors) was on the green screen stage when we spent a grueling day in Edom. Appreciation Friday for the set dec and art department happened in the Institute Chapel as we prepared to shoot the wedding ceremony. Appreciation Sunday for the locations department as we stood on a closed off street in the middle of downtown Toronto ready to stage Jonathan's deadly march toward the Toronto Institute. On the last day, before the gigantic wedding reception, it was appreciation Friday for the cast, all who were there dressed to the nines for the nuptials; Kat, Dom, Alberto, Emeraude, Matt, Harry, Nicola, Paulino, Jack, Jade, Javier, David, Steve, Sydney, Jacky, Ariana. I told them of all the shows I've ever worked on, they were the best group of people I had ever had the pleasure of working with. There was not a bad soul among them, and that was a large part why the fans worldwide loved the show so much. They could sense how special this cast was, as I did that first time I watched on my desktop computer, after I got the call from Jenn Gerstenblatt asking if I had ever seen the show Shadowhunters.

During the entire prep and shoot for the finale, the "Save Shadowhunters" campaign was in full swing on social media, and it was a constant source of inspiration for me. It made me want to share as much as I could with the fandom, and as I headed into the last few days of filming, I declared 48 hours of fan appreciation where I would flood my Twitter feed with pictures and tidbits and try to answer as many questions as I could about the show. I might have gone a little overboard, as evidenced by a few calls from The Powers That Be telling me to chill out. The publicity arm of the network wants to dole out information in a very specific way, and I was getting in the way of that. But I felt an overriding need to share this special, emotional time with the people that were responsible for its success. Those 48 hours came to an end with my two am tweet containing the sad words that every television show must eventually deal with... "And that's a wrap."

# EPILOGUE

*February 27, 2020*
*Los Angeles*
*11:57pm*

The show has been off the air for quite awhile but you'd never know it based on the fandom's social media presence and the awards they still bestow on the show. Thanks to the world of streaming, the episodes can still be watched and enjoyed, and based on some of the Twitter rewatch parties, people are responding like the night it aired. Conventions all over the world continue to draw fans. I was fortunate to be invited to one in New York this coming year, and I'm counting the days.

The cast and crew have all moved on to other projects. Darren and I are working with another group of warm and talented writers, directors, actors and crew members to bring another beloved book series to life. The project is a wonderful experience, but it's not the Shadowhunters experience. No show will ever be as special and dear to my heart, and I think I share that feeling with many other people who worked on the series. It was clear from day one how much this show meant to so many people around the world, and their heartfelt devotion inspired me deeply.

I was blessed to receive an invitation to join the shadow world and be able to move people in ways I never thought possible through a television show. It was the ride of my life and one I knew was entirely unique from my first day on the job. Writing this book helped me memorialize those moments for myself and the rest of the world, every hour spent writing a cathartic reliving of a magical time.

# ACKNOWLEDGEMENTS

Thanks to my wife Tali, who saw the potential in the show before I did when we watched the pilot that fateful summer night on my desktop computer. We have been married forever and she continues to be my rock and the rock of our family. Her patience and support during the endless hours I spent writing this book is much appreciated, even though the volume at which my fingers clack on my keyboard combined with the my cranked Shadowhunters playlist often drove her crazy.

Thanks to my daughters Maya and Cameron, who keep me grounded and humbled like only they can. Thanks to Alyssa McAuliffe, my tireless assistant who has been instrumental in editing and helping me publish this book. And thanks to the graphic designer of the Shadow World, David Nephilim, who I reached out to over Twitter asking if he'd be interested in designing a book cover and a week later it appeared as you see it today.

A very special thank you to Darren William Swimmer, without whom none of this would be possible. Forty years of friendship and thirty years of a professional partnership has given us a treasure trove of wonderful memories. "Harmony and Great Film" is our motto on every show we work on, and Shadowhunters was no different. Darren's editing and thoughts on the book were invaluable.

Lastly, thanks to the fans around the world who were so inspired by the show that they donated a tremendous amount of money and time to various causes in the show's name. You have touched my heart in ways words can't describe. Thank you for being you.

Printed in Great Britain
by Amazon

36394603R00139